SUPER

The Ultimate ▮
to Online B▮

G000153604

SUPERMUMMY™

The Ultimate Mumpreneur's Guide to Online Business Success

Mel McGee

First Published In Great Britain 2009
by www.BookShaker.com

Typeset in Trebuchet

For Terry, Aimee, Emilee and Mickey xxxx

Contents

Acknowledgements

I wish to thank all of the inspirational people, mentors and teachers who have helped to shape my life and influence me in their own unique style. Some of the outstanding people who have shown me the way are:

Tony Robbins, Dan Kennedy, Ali Brown, Melanie Benson-Strick, Lorrie Morgan-Ferrero, Sam Horn and Ari Galper.

To the people whose love, friendship and support have kept me going - Terry, my gorgeous kids, Don, Kathleen, Bev, Gail, Debbie Jenkins and Joe Gregory from - *www.bookshaker.com*. Thank you for believing in me.

To all the amazing mums who follow Supermummy and to everyone who has given me encouragement and shares my vision – Thank you for helping me to make it happen!

Praise for Supermummy

"If only Supermummy had been around when Mumsrock was starting out, well thought-through business advice, delivered in an easy to read style."
Gigi Eligoloff, Founder www.mumsrock.com

"I congratulate Mel on creating this great piece of work. I wish it had been available when I set-up everywoman and my son was just 6 months old. More and more women are setting up ventures from home, often born out of a passion or hobby - It is these types of companies that everywoman believes are the hidden treasure for UK economy."
Karen Gill MBE, Co-founder www.everywoman .com

"Do want to be able to juggle family, life and a business? Mel's highly practical guide can make it a reality– you don't need to read anything else!"
Sue Stockdale, Author of "Secrets of Successful Women Entrepreneurs, www.suestockdale.com

"A really great book for mums considering starting their own business. Some business fundamentals to get you started today to help you talk yourself into it, not out of it!"
Jo Cameron, www.jocameron.co.uk

"Running a business can be a great way to gain flexibility in your life, and many mums take the opportunity of a career break to turn a passion or interest into a business. I hope many more wannabe 'mumpreneurs' take the plunge after gaining valuable advice and tips from the Supermummy book."
Hannah Bourne, www.makeyourmark.org.uk

"Mel McGee has come up with a book that covers not only the big picture around starting your own business, but is also jam packed with vital practical information that means that it's more likely to become a success."
Paula Gardner, www.doyourownpr.com

Foreword

So, you're a mum. Perhaps you're working for somebody else and are tired of the "kids" and "career" juggling act. Maybe you're a first-time mum, ready to head back into the corporate world, but longing for a more flexible career so you can be there for the children. Maybe you've decided to be a full-time mum but you'd like to bring in a second income too? Perhaps you've already started your own business but are in need of a boost from a successful fellow mum-preneur?

How do I know how you feel? Because I'm a mum too. When I first started The Money Gym Phoebe was 4 and Nelson 2, and my husband had just gone back to college to retrain as a sports massage therapist. We were literally living on our credit cards and had just moved in with my sister and her kids to try and cut back our overhead.

Whatever your position now (hopefully better than mine!) I have good news for you - you really can have it all! You can have more income working part-time hours. You can be there 100% for your children while bringing in serious cash from the comfort of your home. And you can do it with less hassle and more certainty now that Mel's book is in your hands. But you're not likely to get that working for somebody else.

So how will you find the ultimate work/life balance solution? By reading this book of course!

Mel really understands the extraordinary demands on both stay at home and working mums. She'll show you new opportunities, new ways of working and a new life style. You'll benefit from expert, easy-to-use information, short cuts, tips, advice and blueprints to help you set up a profitable online business.

As a mum-preneur myself running a successful wealth coaching business I've seen my share of mums who have transformed a good idea into a six and seven figure income. Many have had to do it the hard way. Some have failed. But all of them could have benefited, me included, from reading this book!

Mel McGee aka "Supermummy" shares everything she's learned and sets out a clear and simple roadmap to riches so that you can be a "Supermummy" too!

Nicola Cairncross
Wealth Coach, Professional Speaker & Author
of "The Money Gym", *www.themoneygym.com*

THE NEWS

September 18th 2009

Mumpreneur Phenomenon!

The mumpreneur movement that has silently been gaining momentum in the last few years has now reached a phenomenal peak. Mums throughout the UK are proving to be more resourceful and resilient than ever. An unprecedented 3 out of 5 mums are now making home made profits running businesses that fit around their family life. Becoming a mumpreneur seems to be an inevitable consequence of the frustration felt by so many mums seeking an ideal work/life balance.

Women currently make up 46% of the labour force, by 2010 it's estimated that 1 in 5 workers will be mums. Around 400,000 women take maternity leave each year. Within nine months, 65 percent of women have returned to work, with 21 percent moving to a different employer. After 17 months, 80 percent of women are back at work. In the UK around 30,000 mums are leaving their jobs each year due to pregnancy discrimination.[1]

---

[1] 1HR consultant and researcher, Liz Morris, and the NCT, the UK's leading charity for parents, are embarking on a UK wide survey to gather the experiences of women who have returned to work following maternity leave. Liz Morris, researcher, says; "The demands of caring for a child can be radically different to the demands of the workplace. Women often face realistic anxieties about juggling their new family and their work commitments."

88% of mums working full time would rather work part time or stay at home with their children. The most popular pattern of work is part time employment, but half of all those mums would prefer to have a different role in the family – not just a different job, but a different pattern of life. Although only 8% are self employed, for those that are in this situation it is generally seen as an ideal solution to their needs.[2]

"Women are the largest under-represented group in enterprise. Their untapped talent is essential to Britain's economic competitiveness and productivity. If women started businesses at the same rate as men there would be 150,000 extra start-ups each year in the UK. If we matched US levels of female entrepreneurship there would be 900,000 more businesses in the UK.", Shriti Vadera, Parliamentary Under-Secretary of State for Competitiveness and Small Business.[3]

What does all this really mean? There's no doubt that there are many hard working mums out there putting in long hours because they feel like they have no other choice. Most mums working full time wish that they could be at home more often with the kids and, by comparison, just a few have discovered that the ideal solution is to work for themselves.

Is it any surprise that men start businesses in the UK much more often than women do? It's great that they do and maybe one of the motivating factors for them is to provide for their family but I wonder if they can be more detached about childcare concerns that women. I reckon men and women start businesses primarily for the same reason – to make money but maybe women give more consideration to the impact on family life. Just the thought of ending up tied to a business for sixty hours a week while raising a young family could stop even the most ambitious mum from

---

[2] The Great Work Debate is a survey conducted by Netmums of 4000 mothers of young children. The objectives were to describe the current situation that parents find themselves in, in terms of work, and whether they would prefer to be in a different work pattern.

[3] Taken from her Everywoman Conference speech on 19 November 2008.

giving it her best shot. Let's face it all working mums have a conflict between their commitment to work and family. For a mumpreneur the line between work and family is probably even more blurred but I would suggest that mums working for themselves might be happier with their decision to work than those who feel forced back into working full time.

What about those mums who have returned to a hostile and discriminatory situation at work? I wonder what happens to them after they make the decision to leave such intolerable conditions? Do they become all bitter and twisted from the experience? Does the thought of applying for another job fill them with terror? How does being forced out of work affect their feelings about being a working mum? Can they even be bothered to find the energy and courage to fight back?

Going it alone could be a decision that changes the course of the rest of your life. Deciding to take control and never again settle for less can impact the quality of your life and your family's life – *forever*.

Your desire for a better, different and successful life has brought you to this book. Only you know what success means to you and from where you are now success could be your best revenge. Direct all your frustration, resentment and anger and transform it into energy. A powerful force that will drive you towards taking positive action and getting what you really want. Let them underestimate you and enjoy watching their reaction when they learn about your successful business venture. Wallowing in self pity and moaning about why it's everyone else's fault will get you nowhere. Think how much you will stand out by not only returning to the working world but returning in a blaze of glory as the company Director of your global business. Hey – even if you start from your kitchen table, if you have a website you can reach the world! Smile to yourself as ex colleagues, still bored with their jobs, wonder how on earth you've done it.

Going into business doesn't mean you have to sell your soul. No one is expecting you to impersonate some kind of aggressive control freak? You don't have to go around firing everyone to prove you're the boss. See your feminine side as your strength and recognise what other qualities you may need more of to help you succeed. Each gender has a female and a male energy. It's all about getting the right balance to maintain your feminine and nurturing side while developing a more masculine and powerful side. Let's face it, when it comes to doing business we can learn a thing or two about competitive spirit, thinking big and kicking ass from our men!

I'd like to share a story with you about my first client. When her first baby was six months old she returned to her full time job with mixed feelings of anxiety and curiosity wondering what it was going to be like to be a working mum. Her maternity leave had been spent looking after the needs of her baby and she had given no thought to her options until suddenly she found herself back in a suit at work as if nothing had happened.

She was unprepared for the constant feelings of guilt and worry about leaving her baby for long days at nursery. Although she was performing well and received a promotion she knew that she was not giving her job enough commitment and wondered if she was trying too hard to prove she'd still 'got it'. Feeling trapped and helpless she was secretly relieved to discover she was pregnant again. This time she vowed that she would spend her maternity leave not only meeting the needs of her toddler and new baby but would spend time on her need to find a solution to her work/life balance dilemma.

She knew that only she could change her situation for the better and decided to do whatever it took to avoid being back in the same position but this time with two children depending on her.

She immersed herself in learning and researching and soon she had a plan to start her own business. Her vision became brighter and seemed to move closer as soon as she made the decision to combine her personal passion with her passion for her family.

She found mentors who helped to guide her when she was feeling uncertain. She had to fight with herself to conquer her fears about going it alone, about failing and about not being good enough. She had to convince her husband to back her up and had to hold on firmly to her self-belief when others were not so convinced. She had to resist the impulse to return to work again and finally took the leap of faith to create her new company.

It was so easy to create a new job for herself in her new company, the hard part was creating the right attitude for success. Soon after starting her business she discovered she was pregnant with her third baby. She had to laugh, otherwise she'd cry!

With her new attitude and the advice of her mentors ringing in her ears she stayed on track. To her amazement she realised how far she had come and how she was now stronger and more capable than she ever thought possible. She was running her own business that she created from her home where she had the flexibility to be around more for her kids. She had done it! She had created her ultimate lifestyle by becoming a mumpreneur. Best of all, she has never felt so committed and excited about work as she does working in her Supermummy business. That's right '*she*' is

me! I created Supermummy from a desire to share my passion for growth and contribution with the most important people in the world – mums!

Being a mumpreneur is really all about you creating the ultimate in freedom and flexibility. Forget the work life balance dilemma for once and for all. This is a *lifestyle* choice, it's living your life on your terms, according to your possibilities, not your limitations. I'm you and this is our book.

Entrepreneurs are the unsung heroes of our economy, so whether you are a stay at home mum looking for a new start, working part time wanting a better way to make money or working full time wanting to do a bit of moonlighting before you quit your job - this book will show you how you can do it without breaking the bank!

If you have a burning desire to create a business of your own then go for it! Don't extinguish that fire inside of you. Even after the exhaustion that a new baby brings, if you only have the slightest glow of passion there's hope that it can be ignited.

'We're Having A... Business!'

*"There must be more to life
than having everything."*

MAURICE SENDAK

You'll know when you're getting broody for a business. You can't stop thinking about it. You find yourself gazing at other mumpreneurs with a business longing to be like them. You daydream about what your business would be like. About how much pleasure it will bring to your life. About the wonderful new experiences being a mumpreneur will give you. You can't help feeling as if there is something missing in your life. 'There's got to be more to life than this?' you wonder.

But wait, you don't know anything about being a mumpreneur. You've never been one before. You don't even know if you *can* create a business. Well there's only one way to find out.

Being ready to create your own business manifests as a feeling of *intense desire*. The overwhelming desire you have for a business is your calling to be a mumpreneur and is a signal encouraging you to grow. It might not make logical sense to start a business now. Maybe you think you'll wait until you have more time or more money. You know – the 'right' time. And yes, it's true there never is a 'right' time.

Mums – this is *your* time to go for it. You have the gift of choice and no one else can choose the direction of your life unless you allow them to. It's busy and exhausting at times being a mum and possibly the worst time to start a

1

business. It's also the *best* time to start a business. It's *because of*, not in spite of your kids that you must make decisions and take control of your world. Don't worry about *the* world just focus on *your* world and what you need to do to make *your* world a better place.

Now that you've decided to follow your desire to have a business you are going to need some co-operation from people in your world, especially your partner. They may take a little more convincing...

"Honey, sit down, I've got something to tell you. We're going to have a business! It's going to open up a whole new world for us and with you behind me I know I'll be a great mumpreneur. It's going to take a while before the business is launched so I expect it will take about 9 months of planning, researching and developing before we see any results of all my hard work.

"I'll need to help the new business grow strong by feeding it little and often lots of good things like coaching, marketing, pr, training and organisation. It's going to be tough at first. There might be some sleepless nights while I'm with some new ideas. And don't be upset if I spend more time on the business than you until it becomes less dependant on me. I expect we'll probably wonder what we did with our time before we had the business!

"I'm going to have to learn to be a mumpreneur because I've never done this before. I don't have all the answers and it might be a bit stressful until we adjust to this new way of life.

"This is going to be an exciting journey for us. I am going to grow so much and just imagine how proud we will be to see my little business grow into a big brand. This business is going to change our lives!"

TO WORK OR NOT TO WORK

How did you end up feeling like this in the first place? The chances are you found yourself at the career crossroads or in other words the 'to work or not to work' dilemma. Maybe this is not the first time you have found yourself in this position. Whether this is you first time or last time here your options can seem somewhat limited. If you are completely fulfilled and content with being a full time mum and can't relate to the intense desire to start your own business then this book is not for you.

Perhaps you have a niggling feeling that you would like to do something for yourself and have a different purpose in life, but the feeling hasn't reached intensity because you haven't discovered what it is you want to do – yet!

For most mums at some point, sooner or later the *'When are you going back to work*?' question becomes a harsh reality. A full time job might mean outrageous childcare costs, desperate days agonising about work when your child is ill and a horrible, guilty feeling of just not being there for your kids. Part time might not be so great either especially if you end up in a job for which you are over qualified and underpaid, but put up with because it means you can do the school run.

All this pain and suffering can be good for you! You see sometimes it's only when a situation becomes so unbearable that we start to seek out solutions. Being fed up of resenting work and feeling stuck can be the *driving force* behind the decision to start your own business. The experience of a stressful situation can provide you with opportunities to escape and find a new solution.

Whatever point you are starting from it's important that your entry into the mumpreneur world is a result of a *positive decision* and an *intense desire* to create a new way of living and working.

If you feel forced into starting a business after being made redundant or because your employer can't give you enough flexibility it's unlikely that you will succeed. If you haven't started your business out of desire then you are going to have some emotional baggage to deal with. Avoid seeing your life as the effect of others, which can lead to a place of learned helplessness. If you think that everything that happens in your life is always something or someone else's fault you'll always have an excuse not to do anything about it. You are allowing outside influences to control the direction of your life.

Take responsibility for the family life you really want. See yourself as the cause of great success and experiences coming to you in the future. Best of all you become a role model for your children by showing them what's possible in life. The skills, knowledge, attitude and experience you will gain from business are priceless life skills that you can pass on to your children. Imagine how it will make an impact on them to see you being enterprising and successful as well as being just mum!

FREEDOM FIGHTER

Join the mumpreneur movement and become a freedom fighter! Talk to any mumpreneur and she will tell you that one of the main reasons she started her business was for more flexibility. In other words - *more freedom*.

Freedom works in two ways: freedom *from* something and freedom *to do* something.

The constraints of a full time career, the apathy of a part time job and the weariness of being at home full time with the kids can all be reasons to want to be free of unsatisfying circumstances.

After my first baby daughter I went back to a full time corporate career and became a stressed out working mum preoccupied by needing to leave the office or a meeting on time to make sure I wasn't late picking her up from nursery. Yes, I had an interesting job, a nice salary and time to actually take a lunch break but under the circumstances I felt that I wasn't giving my work as much attention as it deserved and I certainly wasn't giving my daughter as much attention as she deserved.

A couple of years later after my second daughter was born I was in a completely different situation as a full time mum. At first I threw myself into the role of a housewife and mother and it worked for a while probably because I'd convinced myself that I was too exhausted to think any further than the next day. Slowly but surely as my energy came back I realised I was turning into a desperate housewife! By now I was feeling broody – no not for another baby – for a business! I had an intense desire to take control of my work life balance situation for once and for all.

With my maternity leave running out fast and an overdrawn bank account I had no time to waste. I freed myself from the frustration I felt as a full time employee and gave myself the freedom to look for a new opportunity. I took a leap of faith and became a mumpreneur by starting my own business, then discovered I was pregnant with my third baby!

For me having three children and my own business is the ultimate in freedom and flexibility and I've never looked back. Being a mumpreneur has made me stronger and more capable than I ever thought possible. What I am achieving now with three small children would have seemed impossible to me only a few years ago after having my first baby. Having won the battle for the freedom to have my own business and be there for my kids I'm not going to give it up without a fight!

What's so great about being a mumpreneur is that I am now the best employee that I have ever been! I am more focussed, committed, creative, determined and ambitious now that I'm the boss. There is no room for complacency and apathy in your own business and your success will be a direct result of your efforts. Don't fool yourself into thinking that just deciding to start your own business alone is going to change your life. For you and your family to enjoy the rewards of your business success you must *consistently* work at it.

That doesn't mean night after night burning the midnight oil and burning your-self out. It means making a commitment to block time daily to implement your plan. Okay I know you want to free yourself from the 9-5-thank-God-it's-Friday routine and that'll work only if you find a way to look after your business. Not sure how? You don't need to know the how at this stage, just keep reading!

Back to being a freedom fighter. Use this table to help you to clarify what you want freedom from and what you want freedom to do:

I WANT FREEDOM FROM...	I WANT FREEDOM TO DO...

NO IF'S NO BUTS YOU CAN DO IT!

Excuses, excuses! You've got the intense desire, you know what you want freedom from and freedom to do so what's stopping you from going for it?

Haven't got the time, haven't got the money, haven't got the experience, haven't got the confidence?

Excuses like these are simply a smokescreen. What you haven't got is *belief*. Now let's not underestimate the power of beliefs. Your beliefs can create and destroy any experience of your life. Don't allow any negative, limiting beliefs you have about yourself to destroy your chance of business success. When you believe something what you really have is a feeling of *certainty* about something. For you to have formed that certainty you must have evidence to support why you think it's true. Take a positive belief you may have about yourself for example *"I'm a good mum"* – what supporting evidence do you have to believe that? Perhaps people have told you that you are a good mum, maybe your children tell you they love you and that's what makes you believe you are a good mum, or giving your children some undivided attention feels like being a good mum. Whatever the reasons what's important is that you know how you have formed that belief about yourself.

For you to achieve mumpreneur success you are going to need to believe that:

- You *must* do it
- You *can* do it

Whether you are motivated to start your own business out of inspiration or desperation what's important is that you are *moving towards* your goal. To get some leverage remind yourself of all the *compelling reasons* why you must take action. You need to be in a position where you believe it's possible. You don't know what your limits are until you reach them and you will never know what you were *truly capable* of if you don't try.

Next you have to believe that you can do it. Think about the evidence you must have to support a belief. At this point if you are questioning your belief about being capable of running a successful business challenge where your evidence for that belief has come from. Who put that into your mind? What has been said or done to you in the past to make you believe that? Now *reject* that belief as an old belief.

To be a mumpreneur you must be open to creating new, empowering beliefs about what you can achieve. I'll start you off with this one:

> *"You are stronger and more capable*
> *than you ever thought possible"*

The only way you can prove that you are capable of achieving something is when you actually achieve it. Until then you don't know for certain so it's much better to have the belief that you can. You can't prove that you cannot achieve something when you've never tried so you can only say that you haven't achieved it *yet*.

To make a breakthrough with changing your negative beliefs you need to understand how this is *hurting* you. How are you suffering now and what effect will these beliefs have on your future if you don't change them now? Here's how you can start changing the way you talk about your capabilities:

> *"I'm not experienced in business yet"*

> *"I don't know about sales an*
> *marketing at the moment"*

*"In the past, I have been indecisive
about taking control of situations"*

"If-then" beliefs are another effective way to strengthen empowering beliefs:

*"If I focus on growing my business
consistently then I will succeed"*

*"If I'm enthusiastic and open to opportunities
then I will attract success"*

Even if you have no evidence of previous successes or achievements it's still possible for you to create a belief that you can succeed. In NLP there is a belief that *"The past does not equal the future"*. This means that no matter what has happened in your life before you can start from today believing that you can achieve business success. All you have to do is use your imagination, visualise and have faith that what you see happening will happen.

 **SUPERTIP**

Don't accept that because you are now a mum you are somehow less of a person. Having your children (your greatest achievement) has not limited you and your confidence has not been lost somewhere (where did it go?)

All great leaders and people who have achieved outstanding success know the power of having vision. Be optimistic and believe that wonderful opportunities *will* come to you. There is only so much you can plan for in business. If you believe you can do it you will find a way or *the way will find you*.

KEY POINTS

- Being ready to create your own business manifests as a feeling of intense desire.
- The overwhelming desire you have for a business is your calling to be a mumpreneur and is a signal encouraging you to grow.
- You have the gift of choice and no one else can choose the direction of your life unless you allow them to.
- Don't worry about *the* world just focus on *your* world and what you need to do to make *your* world a better place.
- Being fed up of resenting work and feeling stuck can be the driving force behind the decision to start your own business.
- Whatever point you are starting from it's important that your entry into the mumpreneur world is a result of a positive decision and an intense desire to create a new way of living and working.
- The skills, knowledge, attitude and experience you will gain from business are priceless life skills that you can pass on to your children.
- Freedom works in two ways: freedom from something and freedom to do something.
- There is no room for complacency and apathy in your own business and your success will be a direct result of your efforts.
- You do not know what your limits are until you reach them and you will never know what you were truly capable of if you don't try.
- Don't allow any negative, limiting beliefs you have about yourself to destroy your chance of business success.

- The only way you can prove that you are capable of achieving something is when you actually achieve it.
- No matter what has happened in your life before you can start from today believing that you can achieve business success.
- If you believe you can do it you will find a way or the way will find you.

The BIG Idea

*"Money never starts an idea,
it's the idea that starts the money."*

MARK VICTOR HANSEN CO-AUTHOR
OF CHICKEN SOUP FOR THE SOUL

So now you are convinced that you want to be a mumpreneur and you're all pumped up with self-belief you need a BIG idea. Even if you've already got an idea up your sleeve don't be tempted to skip this section because it's possible that your idea can make you or it can break you. You could save yourself a lot of pain and misery not to mention time and money by getting it 'right' from the start.

Before we get into ideas let's take stock of you. What do you bring to the party? Design your business from day one to play to your strengths.

Start from *where* you are with *what* and *who* you know now and grow to where you *ideally* want to be.

- What are your best skills?
- What do you know you are good at?
- What have people said you are good at?
- What do you know that is specialist or unusual or interesting to others?
- What knowledge do you have that could be used to provide solutions to certain problems?
- Who do you know from the past or present that could be a useful resource to you?
- How could those people help you?

This exercise will help you to do a personal stock take.

MY PERSONAL STOCK TAKE

My Skills	My Knowledge	Who I know

Being a mum with children dependant on you it's possible that you might feel uncomfortable with the idea of the reckless, risk taking entrepreneur stereotype. There is no need to put unnecessary pressure on your-self. You don't have to re-mortgage the house and cash in your life savings to start a business.

While it's true that starting a business is a risk due to uncertainty your objective is to manage the risk. You're used to that already. Just think how many times a day you are managing risk at home with the kids without even realising it!

To be a mumpreneur means taking calculated risks. Your start up costs could come from various sources and there could be many creative ways for you to get what you need. You can always start small and think BIG. As you gradually develop the skills of a risk managing mumpreneur you can make bigger decisions about your business.

The most important key at the idea stage of your business is that you can get your idea out there fast, that it has room to grow in the future and that you don't limit yourself.

WHAT NOT TO DO

Dreaming up your business idea is great fun. Once you get started you'll be coming up with the most weird and wonderful ways to go into business. I call this brainstorming phase the '*What about...?*' stage because you'll find yourself constantly asking your partner, friends, kids, "*What about a soft play centre just for mums and dads?*" or "*What about potty training courses?*" and watching for their reaction. By the way this is not classified as market research!

What's your big idea? If you don't have one yet – great! You will avoid getting hooked on a business idea that may not give you the results you really want. If you already have a big idea you'll find many ways here to market your idea, sell your idea or adapt your idea.

The deal is that you need to get going with your idea. Get it out there – *fast*. You haven't got the time or energy for trial and error and a slow, frustration slog to profitability. Don't wait until you have made the perfect decision either. Stay flexible because you can adapt your idea as you go. To give yourself the best chance of success and a competitive advantage go *against* what the majority are doing. Although it's good to model your business on other successful businesses avoid becoming just a '*me-too*' version. Deliberately choose to do the opposite of what is considered 'the norm'. That's one of the reasons why entrepreneurs have the potential to be so successful.

From now on start thinking like a mumpreneur. Your purpose for going into business must be to make money –

simple. Of course you want to enjoy making money by doing something that interests you and keeps you stimulated but you must keep the purpose of making money at the front of your mind. Your business is not about keeping you occupied; it's about making profits to reward you for all the risk and effort you put in. You owe it to yourself to succeed.

Beware of going into business simply because it's always something you wanted to do. The market doesn't care that you've dreamed about being a wedding planner ever since your best friend's wedding! No offence to wedding planners! They only care about what you can offer or do to help them or solve a problem.

Think long and hard about your reason. Now think about what's different about your business. Your objective must be to stand out not blend in. Where is the space for you? You need to carve out a place for your business in the marketplace that makes you *appear* to be unique. The fact is that there is nothing completely new, instead there are improved, adapted and re-invented versions.

Why make it hard for yourself by trying to compete in a crowded market? Could you offer a product or service relating to a trend? People will always be interested in something interesting and fresh. Maybe you could try a really unconventional approach and enter the market causing surprise and awe.

How often do you get irritated by bad service? It's a sad but true fact that experiencing great service is the exception rather than the rule these days. Your business could stand apart from others simply by you deciding to raise and maintain the standards of your business far higher than the current, accepted standards.

The purpose of this is to invest time wisely now to giving your business the best chance possible to be outstanding when you launch. Get it right from the start and it will be much easier for you to promote what you do, get noticed and have people recommend you by word-of-mouth.

DON'T JUST THINK IT, INK IT

Sitting down with a piece of paper and willing yourself to come up with ideas is not the best way to get inspiration. You need to give yourself some space for your creative thoughts to flow. Anyway you're a busy mum and haven't got the luxury of shutting yourself away in a retreat or taking yourself off to the top of a mountain to contemplate ideas for your business.

Back in the real world you'll need to find a way to capture your best thoughts as and when they come to you. Even a simple notebook to hand will be adequate to keep a record of your random ideas. Watch out - because from now on you are going to experience great surges of inspirational ideas flashing through your mind like a bolt of lightening. In the car, at the school gate, strolling around the supermarket, in your dreams, in the shower, on the toilet!

Your creative thoughts are indiscriminate and are there to guide you. Don't waste time analysing whether an idea will or won't work, whether a business name is right, if a domain name is a good fit at this stage just make a note of everything. You have to allow your conscious thinking to filter down into your unconscious mind and wait for the rich, most powerful ideas to flow. They will come and present themselves to you as a niggle, a hunch or an 'aha!' Get it written down as quickly as possible. You don't have to understand how it fits into your business right now. Just trust that all your most creative thoughts and ideas will soon start to take the shape of a viable business.

If you've already had some great ideas or get some as you read this book make a note of them here.

MY BRIGHT IDEAS

GIVE US A CLUE

Not sure where to start? Look for *gaps* in the market. Open your eyes. Listen to what people around you are talking about. Pick up on problems people have and explore what solutions you could provide. Once you are open to opportunity you will find a way or *the way will find you*. When you start thinking like an entrepreneur you'll start to see many ways that you could provide a product or service.

You must be open to any possibility and opportunity from this point forwards. What can happen at this stage is you instantly come up with 10 great business ideas! That's okay – give yourself some time and see which ideas keeping coming back to you. With each idea you don't need to start writing out a business plan but you do need to ask yourself *'Where is the profit?'* Evaluate each idea for its money making potential.

Once you have an idea you now have to identify who you are going to market to – your target market. There are thousands of potential niche markets out there. Before you start thinking about your business idea for a product or service you must identify a niche target market.

You need to position yourself so that you are the one a potential customer in your niche thinks about. Choose a market that you have a natural affinity with so that you can relate to your customers. Who do you understand, talk the same language as, have empathy with? Pay attention and listen to them so you can figure out what they really want. Knowing what they want and marketing to those desires will put you in a powerful position.

This exercise will help you to select a hot target market.

MY HOT TARGET MARKET

1. Which different groups of people do you have an affinity with?
2. Identify an individual from one of your groups. Give them a name and write as much as possible about them. For example gender, age, occupation, income bracket, geographic location, marital status, kids, pets, cars, hobbies etc.
3. What are some of the problems, wants, needs and desires of your target market?
4. Which of the above is the biggest issue? What really keeps them awake at night? What problem would they be willing to spend money on the most?

5. What products and/or services could you provide to solve this problem?

When it comes down to deciding on a name for your business choose a name that shouts what you do to attract the customers you want. It might sound basic now but go into your local town and notice how many business signs there are that do not instantly tell you what the business is all about. A business with a name that means nothing is harder to market than a name that telegraphs the service. Think about the industry you are going into and how you can gain a competitive edge with your business name.

THE 3 MUMPRENEUR MARKETING MISTAKES AND HOW TO AVOID THEM

Mistake 1 – Deciding on a product or service first.

Most marketers decide on the product or service first, create it or find it then have to try and find a market to sell it to. It's hard work constantly trying to create a demand and get people to buy from you. A much better and easier way is to identify a hot target market. Find out what the people want and supply a product or service that gives them what they want. So find the *demand first* then supply.

Mistake 2 – Kidding yourself that they need your product or service.

One of the problems with people is they don't always want what they need! Take diets for example. Some people need to go on a diet but they don't want to. How about exercise? Many people need to take more exercise but they don't want to. Your customers are only human just like you!

To get people to respond to you and what you are offering you need to give messages that match their wants. In general people want to: save time, save money, look better, feel better, be healthier, have more convenience, get things quickly and easily, have more money and more time, get better service and, better quality etc. You are selling the *benefits* of your product or service according to the wants of your target market.

Mistake 3 – Thinking doing what you are passionate about is enough to make money.

Yes it's essential to your success that you enjoy what you are doing and it's true that it's possible to become wealthy by doing something you love. The key word here is *enough*. It's not enough to simply love what you do and expect people to hear about you and come knocking on your door! You must be able to spread the word effectively about what you do to the people who are most likely to buy from you. Being a starving artist is not a good business! Go ahead and create that masterpiece if that is what you love but get it done and go all out to *attract* the right buyers for it with a marketing strategy. Or better still get a commission paid in advance then go ahead and create your masterpiece!

To help you be sure your business idea is right for you and will give you the freedom and flexibility you want test it against these criteria:

- Product or service people need or desire
- Low start up costs
- Low running costs – location, staff, stock etc
- Little or no competition
- Uses your skills or knowledge
- Payment upfront
- Unlimited global market

- Fits around your family life
- Mobile – can work from any location
- Gives you satisfaction
- Ability to adapt if required

SUPERTIP

Once you have decided on a great name for your
business buy the matching domain name.

THE 7 STEPS TO MUMPRENEUR SUCCESS

Run your idea through these seven steps to test how it
will work at each step.

7. GROW & EXPAND
Repeat what works to grow your income

6. SYSTEMS
Use systems to be more effective and productive

5. MONEY
Get recurring and upfront payment

4. PLAN
Devise marketing and sales strategy

3. TEAM
Get the right people to help you run your business

2. BRAND
Give your idea a name and an identity

1. IDEA
Devise a unique product or service people want and need

BASIC INSTINCT

Sixth sense, intuition, gut feeling – all ways of describing one very important part of your decision making process – using your *instincts*. We are born with natural instincts for a reason. They are there to guide us and protect us. Sometimes we make decisions not based on facts, intelligence or logic but because of the powerful feelings that our instinct gives us. Learn to trust your instinct because it will serve you well when you are running your business and needing to make so many decisions for yourself.

It may be your instinct telling you to go for a particular idea. You know it in your heart or you feel it in your gut that it's the right business for you. Get your idea out of your head and out there. Some people love thinking up ideas but never act on them. It's great fun to dream about your ideas but if you never turn them into a tangible product or service they will never become a profitable reality. You can't make any money from an idea in your head. Just start from where you are now with what you've got and get going.

Or, imagine where you ideally want to be with your business and work backwards to where you are now. Only you can make it happen. If it means giving the sofa a rest in the evenings while you get started so be it! You have to *take action* on your idea.

KEY POINTS

- You could save yourself a lot of pain and misery not to mention time and money by getting it 'right' from the start.
- You can start from where you are with what and who you know now and grow to where you ideally want to be.
- Being a mumpreneur means taking calculated risks.
- The most important key at the idea stage of your business is that your idea has room to grow in the future and that you don't limit yourself.
- From now on start thinking like a mumpreneur. You are an entrepreneurial mum and your purpose for going into business must be to make money – simple.
- Stay flexible because you can adapt your idea as you go.
- To give your-self the best chance of success and a competitive advantage and go against what the majority are doing.
- Your objective must be to stand out not blend in. Where is the space for you? You need to carve out a place for your business in the marketplace that makes you appear to be unique.
- Get it right from the start and it will be much easier for you to promote what you do, get noticed and have people recommend you by word-of-mouth.
- Just trust that all your most creative thoughts and ideas will soon start to take the shape of a viable business.
- Don't waste time analysing whether an idea will or won't work, whether a business name is right, if a domain name is a good fit at this stage just make a note of everything as and when it comes to you.

- Evaluate your idea for money making potential.
- Identify a hot target market. Find out what the people want and supply a product or service that gives them what they want.
- You are selling the benefits of your product or service according to the wants of your target market.
- It's not enough to simply love what you do and expect people to hear about you and come knocking on your door!
- It's great fun to dream about your ideas but if you never turn them into a tangible product or service they will never become a profitable reality.
- Trust your instinct.

Success Mindset

*"Luck is What Happens When
Preparation Meets Opportunity."*

SENECA

To be prepared for success means you must be *ready* to receive success and that means you must *believe* that success is coming to you. Easier said than done!
You must develop the ability to boost your own self-belief and self esteem to succeed. Without realising it you may even be sabotaging your chances right now with feelings of self-doubt.

Allow me to introduce you to your best friend, your worst enemy and your super power– *your mind*! It's essential to your success that you understand how your mind works and the differences between your conscious and unconscious minds.

Conscious mind – is the mind that you use very day to *actively* think about what you do and say. The conscious mind is limited and can only hold small amounts of information at any one time. Most of what you say and do is run automatically by your unconscious mind

Unconscious mind – processes information every second from all of your senses. It stores all your memories and is the source of your creativity. Throughout your life you have been conditioned to think, speak and behave in a certain way – mostly without realising. You have created 'habits' for yourself that your unconscious mind now runs for you *automatically* which frees up your conscious mind to do other things.

The only way to overcome your unconscious conditioning is to re-train yourself by practising new ways of thinking, saying and doing until they are your new habits. Habits that you have *purposefully* chosen for yourself.

SUPERTIP

Think of your mind as being like your 'super power'.
An invisible and powerful force that controls your thoughts, your behaviour, your imagination and your inner voice.

Ok back to reality now. It's okay to go around with your head in the clouds as long as you keep your feet on the ground. Believing in yourself is a must but is not enough for you to succeed. You are going to need a whole new mindset to be a mumpreneur. A mindset for success. All of your great ideas, planning, research and effort will be wasted if you neglect to develop and grow the way you think. Contrary to popular belief having the best education, qualifications, state-of-the-art offices, most innovative product, most experience or a huge chunk of investment does not guarantee success. The *person or people* in the business are the key factor for success or failure.

Remember your business has one primary purpose – to make you money. You haven't started a business just for something to do or to have something to talk about at the school gates. To be a successful mumpreneur you must start thinking like an entrepreneur. The skill of an entrepreneur is to create profitable businesses in any way they choose. That's the beauty of being a mumpreneur because the 'how' you make money is your choice.

Succeeding as a mumpreneur is going to require commitment and determination. Don't think of your business as something you are just dabbling in until you find a 'proper job' when the kids are older!

Take your new mumpreneur identity seriously and purposefully seek out people you can learn from to *master* the entrepreneurial attitude you need.

Resilience + Resourcefulness + Re-inventing yourself + Responsibility for your success + Role Models to inspire you = Rewards

 **SUPERTIP**

Changing your attitude is like magic. Your whole world will change too and it's so much easier to cope with life with the 'right' attitude.

GETTING IN WITH THE RIGHT CROWD

There's no doubt that we are greatly influenced by our peer group. As an aspiring mumpreneur you may not yet have formed relationships with people who can help you to improve your business attitude and aptitude.

Business philosopher Jim Rohn says, *"Character isn't something you were born with and can't change, like your fingerprint. It's something you weren't born with and must take responsibility for forming."*

One of the issues you are likely to face to some degree in your ambition to be a mumpreneur is lack of support from the people in your life. It's going to be a real test of your resilience and self-belief when you spend time with people who are sceptical, critical, fearful or silently disapprove of your business idea. Hopefully you will find that other people encourage you, support you and inspire you, which will help to offset the negative effects from the doom-and-gloomers.

It's important to understand that their negative reaction may be based in fear. They may be afraid for you of your business failing, they may be afraid of what might happen to your relationship with them if you succeed, they may even be afraid that *they* will never find something to get so excited about as you have done.

You may also discover that suddenly everyone is an expert on business and is more than happy to give you their advice about what you should or shouldn't do! When I realised what was going on I found it particularly entertaining and made a decision that I would only follow the advice of those who were already running successful businesses.

So what does all this mean? Well it means you must be cautious about what and who you allow to affect you. From now on you must make it a daily habit to feed your mind with inspiration, motivation, stimulation, big ideas and new opportunities. Cut out the junk like boring TV, mind numbing gossip magazines and time spent with people who drag you down. Be more selective about what messages out there you allow to affect your thinking. If you only choose to hear and respond to all the negativity in the world that will become your reality – you'll create your own world of worry. What we are not good at is seeing the positive in the world. Every day, all over the world babies are being born, people's lives are being saved, celebrations are taking place and acts of love and kindness are everywhere.

Put yourself on the Supermummy Power diet!

THE SUPERMUMMY POWER DIET

Cut Out	Take in Moderation	Enjoy Unlimited
Moaning	Advice from non-experts	Motivation
Whinging	Reality checks	Stimulation
Excuses	Constructive criticism	Inspiration
Criticism	A break from	Advice from experts
Scepticism	it all to relax	Visualising
Fear		Self-belief
Jealousy		Determination
Resentment		Courage
Self pity		Admiration of success

Your performance and mindset are going to be greatly affected by whom you choose to associate with. You don't necessarily need to physically hang around with a person to be influenced by them. Think about books you've read, characters you've seen in film or stories you may have heard that have inspired you in some way. It's possible for you to find the guidance you need from so many different resources.

You can avoid the isolation and increase your chances of success by seeking out a group, network or organisation of like-minded entrepreneurs to invest in. That's why coaching groups work so well because every one shares the same goal for success and mastery.

If you're wondering where to find a place for you take a look at *www.supermummy.com*. The Supermummy Inner Circle membership program is especially for aspiring and established mumpreneurs.

Top Tip: If you feel yourself getting into a state of worry sit up, keep your head up, breathe deeply for a while and remain still. Don't allow yourself to 'do' worry.

DON'T JUST LEARN IT – MASTER IT

If you want to master something *do* it – over and over again. Read books about it, talk to people who have already done it, learn from people who are great at it, fail at it a few times. It's like being a parent for the first time. You can read all the books and listen to all the advice but it's when your new baby arrives that the learning really begins!

I use the principle of mastery to guide me in my own business and want to share this secret with you. The point at which you must make the decision to master something is when you have applied yourself to learning a skill and then reach a kind of plateau. The learning has ceased and although you are still putting time in you have stopped making progress. At this point the 'dabbler' will decide to give up, the 'stressor' decides to fight for success and achieves their goal eventually but is too exhausted to enjoy it.

The better way is to take the path of mastery. When you are on the path to mastery you expect to reach a plateau at various points in your progress so there's no reason to stress out when it happens. Accept where you are and seek out someone who knows the path ahead and can show you the way to mastery. Following these three simple steps, will help you to master any new skill.

MUMPRENEUR MASTERY
IN 3 SIMPLE STEPS

Step 1: Find someone outstanding who is already successful at the highest level and model yourself on them. Ask yourself "What would X do?" Get yourself a coach or mentor to support you.

Step 2: Immerse yourself – to be a master you must first be a student – never stop learning.

Step 3: Repetition, repetition, repetition – until you have mastered it!

Here's an exercise to help you see how easy it can be to master something.

COULDN'T THEN – CAN NOW

Think about skills that you have learned in your life. List 3 things that you once thought you couldn't do, like driving, which are easy to do now.

1. _____

2. _____

3. _____

Okay so to master these skills all you need to do is make a commitment to improve, immerse yourself in learning and consistently make progress until you have mastered it for yourself.

Now list 3 things that you can't do (yet!) and would like to master.

1. _____

2. _____

3. _____

This exercise is a reminder for you that you have already mastered new skills and achieved success in something that once you thought was impossible.

FROM A TO B

When it comes to promoting yourself you can be your own best friend or your worst enemy. What's getting in your way of moving forward with your business and putting yourself 'out there'? Fear.

Fear of failure, fear of disappointment, fear of criticism, fear of rejection, fear of judgement, fear of success and ultimately fear that you are not good enough.

This is where excuses come from. We are afraid to do something like start a business and instead of admitting that we come up with all kinds of reasons why we can't do it, like:

"I'd love to but I haven't got the time"

"I just can't see it working"

"Mums aren't the right sort of people to run businesses"

Being in a state of fear could destroy your chances of business success before you've even handed out your first business card!

Fear is a natural instinct, it's there to protect you and there is nothing you can do to take your fear away.

Want to know a secret? Everyone feels fear, even multi-millionaires! Accept that feeling fear is a part of the process of doing something new. Fear is energy. It's a powerful force, which can either paralyse you or propel you into taking action.

Don't try to fight fear instead learn to live with it. Achieving business success is going to mean getting out of your comfort zone and putting yourself into new and awkward situations. You were probably afraid of giving birth and look at the amazing result you have from going through that terrifying experience!

Surely it's better to do something, have a go, and learn from 'mistakes' than to stay paralysed by fear? You can learn a great deal about conquering fear simply by watching your children. Remember when they were learning to walk? How they would take a few steps then tumble down, sometimes hurting themselves, yet that did not stop them from getting back up determined to try again. Sure enough it didn't take long for them to be toddling around like a little chimp all over the place. Children haven't been conditioned to be fearful in the same way that adults have. Yet nothing worthwhile would be accomplished if we didn't have the courage to act, despite the fear.

Here's an exercise to help you deal with some of the fears that might be holding you back.

NO FEAR

Thinking about your business, what are 3 of your greatest fears?

1. _____

2. _____

3. _____

Now ask yourself...

"What might happen if I did...?"

"How is feeling... about... helping me to achieve success?"

"What's the worst that can happen if I do...?"

Now that you can relax knowing that it's okay to be afraid why not make it easier and quicker for yourself to reach your goals?

FAKING IT

Imagine you are at the bottom of a ladder, which represents your business. Right now you are standing at the bottom. What are you going to do next? Are you looking at the ground imagining the blood, sweat and tears it's going to take to claw your way to the top? In our society we have been conditioned to associate career success with climbing the ladder. With this on your mind it's easy to understand why you might slowly take your first step at the bottom anticipating the long climb ahead. *"But at least I've taken the first step"* you cry, *"The only way is up."*

Yes that's true but what's also true is that now you are the boss you can promote yourself straight to the top of the ladder. You are not at the mercy of someone else's opinion about whether you deserve to be there or have to stay where you are until they give you permission to climb up another step. You make up the rules for your business and now you are the Director you go straight to the top of the ladder from day one!

It's important that you present the image for yourself and your business as being at the top right from the start. In NLP this is called the *'as-if'* frame of reference and means acting *'as-if'* you had already achieved the business success you desire. In other words pretend you are a successful mumpreneur at the top of the ladder before you actually get there!

If it's not necessary to tell someone that you have only been in business for a week then just don't tell them. I'm not suggesting that you go out and buy a flash new wardrobe, sports car, bigger house to pretend to be rich when really you have taken on loads more debt. What you are doing here is tricking yourself into thinking like and acting like a successful entrepreneur.

It's the perception that others have of you and your business that makes the difference. Give the perception that your business is bigger like using a few different e-mail addresses or pretending you are the PA when you answer the phone or make business calls. It just might take a while for your profits to catch you up!

You might think that it will take some time until you have built up your confidence and 'earned' that position. If you're not convinced yet to try this out then think about it in terms of time. You are a busy mum running a business. The quicker you can get yourself started, get business and start making money the better. Why bother putting yourself through a long and frustrating slog to the top? Remember the old rules don't apply any more. How good are you going to feel imagining yourself as already at the top compared to struggling at the bottom? Exactly!

The '*as-if*' frame is effective for problem solving too because you can't solve a problem with the same thinking that created it. Ask yourself, "*If I was already a successful mumpreneur what would I do to solve this problem*?" When we try to solve a problem from our current circumstances and way of thinking we often limit our options and acting '*as-if*' helps you to access new, more powerful ways of problem solving.

IN LIMBO

Transition is one of the most difficult times you will experience in your business. You have taken a leap of faith and left your old position but have not yet attained the benefits of the new position. It's an uncomfortable place to be.

Don't dwell on the negative things, what might go wrong.
Think about the rewards and how good you'll feel.

This could be a frightening time of self- doubt and panic so expect it and don't let your dream die. It's up to you to breathe life into it. Once you are past the excitement of coming up with your big idea you'll begin to question whether you are doing the right thing and you might even start to think that the 9-5-thank-God-it's-Friday work routine isn't so bad after all!

Common doubts include:

- Did I opt out of getting a job because I don't think I can hack it anymore?
- Is starting a business really just a cop out?
- Can I really cope with running a business? At least it's easier to just turn up, work, get paid and go home.
- Am I just kidding myself?
- Are my friends who are at home with the kids and/working for someone else right? Will I isolate myself too much if I spend time starting and running a business? What will they think of me if I become really successful?
- Why am I not happy anyway? Why do I want to do this? Shouldn't I be fulfilled enough being a stay at home mum?

Doubts like these can only invade your mind if there is nothing else to fill it. When the mind lacks an external focus it turns inward on itself. You might also get so fed up that you just give up on your business dream. This is *not* thinking like a mumpreneur. Stay focussed on your business ambition. Get going with it and those nagging doubts will disappear.

KEY POINTS

- You are going to need a whole new mindset to be a mumpreneur. A mindset for success.
- Succeeding as a mumpreneur is going to require commitment and determination.
- It's going to be a real test of your resilience and self-belief when you spend time with people who are sceptical, critical, fearful or just silently disapprove of your business idea.
- You must be cautious about what and who you allow to affect you.
- It's possible for you to find the guidance you need from so many different resources.
- Accept where you are and seek out someone who knows the road and can show you the way to mastery.
- Fear is a natural instinct, it's there to protect you and there is nothing you can do to take your fear away.
- Don't try to fight fear instead learn to live with it because achieving business success is going to mean getting out of your comfort zone and putting yourself into new and awkward situations.
- You make up the rules for your business and if you want to position yourself at the top of the ladder from day one then good for you!
- It's the perception that others have of you and your business that makes the difference.
- Remember the old rules don't apply any more.
- Doubts can only invade your mind if there is nothing else to fill it.

Time Management

"Don't tell me about the labour pains,
just show me the baby."

MICHAEL LEE AUSTIN

So you've been having a great time so far dreaming up your business idea and imagining yourself running your successful global business from the kitchen table. Let's get a reality check here! Being a mumpreneur with family and business commitments to meet simultaneously is easier said than done. The difference between your business going nowhere and going places is implementation. Just like the ironing won't get done by itself, your business won't run itself.

There is a lot you can do to automate your business to save you time but ultimately you need to work out a system for managing your time. You need to dramatically change your relationship with time so that you consistently work on growing your business and avoid overwhelm. What can happen when we feel overwhelmed is that we tell ourselves that there is so much to do, that we just don't know where to start, so we put it off for now and end up wasting time by watching TV or going shopping. This is where it all goes wrong because now we are rewarding ourselves for not doing tasks by doing something we'd rather do like watch TV. Then the next day it starts all over again and now we feel guilty that we haven't done X, Y, or Z.

It's the same principle we are likely to use when we would like our children to accomplish a task – we reward them – with praise or a gold star. How about if you rewarded your child for not doing something by letting them watch TV and eat sweets?

SuperTip

If you are feeling overwhelmed and things have really got out of hand, split up all the things that need doing into smaller chunks and do small tasks on a daily basis.

It doesn't have to be mission impossible when you know how. You're a busy mum with both your kids and your business to look after and the demands on your time are extraordinary so you *must* take extraordinary measures to cope.

You may have read or been trained in time management theory and strategy before which can be applied to the 9-5-thank-God-it's-Friday routine, but most of that doesn't apply to your life as a mumpreneur. One of the best reasons for starting your own business is for a healthier work/life balance so start conditioning yourself from day one to be more effective and productive.

Now you are your own boss it's down to you to make your business a success in however many hours you choose. Time is a precious asset – you need time to think, plan, create, solve problems and, communicate. And you only have 24 hours a day. So it's not about the *quantity* of time you have to spend on your business it's the *quality*.

From now on be aware of how you are using your time, wasting your time and allowing others to waste your time. Make a habit of checking in with your-self by asking, "*Am I being productive?*" or "*How is spending time on this task contributing to profitability?*" Be curious about how other business people manage to get everything done and make it your business to find out. Instead of exclaiming, *"I don't know how she does it!"* think to your-self, *"I must find out how she does it!"*

PARKINSON AND PARETO

No it's not a new talk show! Understanding Parkinson's Law and Pareto's Law gives you a great advantage when it comes to getting things done. Each has it's own merits but when used together you could get more achieved in 20 minutes that you used to get done in a whole day!

Parkinson's Law says that a task will increase in importance in relation to the time allowed for it's completion – meaning that a task will take as much time as you allow for it. Give yourself a week to do something and it'll take a week. Give yourself the same task to do in a day and it'll only take a day.

This is why deadlines work and you *must* create a habit of setting deadlines for yourself to work on your business. The pressure to meet a deadline increases productivity and the closer the deadline the more energy and focus you put into the task. Some of what you need to do will have a deadline set by another person but as you are your own boss now you must get into the habit of setting deadlines for yourself. How? Get a big clock right next to your work-space and give yourself specific time slots to work to. Another way is to set a timer to an hour, 20 minutes or whatever time you have, then give the task 100% focus.

Identify the 20% of your tasks that contribute the most to your business then give yourself short deadlines to implement them.

Pareto's Law says that 80% of the outputs come from 20% of the inputs. Also known as the 80/20 principle it can be applied to various contexts such as:

- 80% of your sales come from 20% of your customers
- 80% of your results come from 20% of the effort and time

If you don't do anything else about your time management just apply this one strategy routinely to your business to see the best results:

Here's an exercise to help you clarify what tasks you need to focus on now and what might be stopping you from taking action.

JUST DO IT

Think about what you must do now to make progress. In no particular order list the tasks that need to be done then write down the reason why that task is important and the reason why it hasn't been done yet.

What Must I Do?	Why Must I Do It?	What's Stopping Me?

TIME IS MONEY

It's generally more difficult for women to set boundaries for ourselves and as a mum it's only natural that you want to be more available to meet the needs of your family. Where do you draw the line and get the courage to enforce your boundaries? You can only be your best when you get the time you need. It's for the benefit of your family too because they are the ones who'll suffer the most when you are overwhelmed, exhausted and irritable.

Start taking your time seriously from day one. Traditional time management theory for placing an hourly value on time for a full time job works like this:

Annual income figure ÷ 220 work days ÷ 8 = hourly rate

Now the problem here is that we all know that employees don't put in 8 hours of *productive* time every day. Out of those 8 hours how much time is spent settling in to the office in the morning, chatting by the water cooler, checking personal e-mail or browsing the internet, making personal phone calls, attending meetings for meetings and being distracted by colleagues?

As a mumpreneur you probably won't have a standard work day or work week. You have *time* and the time you have to work on your business *must* be the most focussed and productive of all. You'll be amazed at how much can be achieved in just an hour a day of productive time.

When you start your business it's going to be difficult for you to evaluate how much your time is really worth when you may be putting in many hours to get to a point when you can pay yourself. To get the same results as an eight hour day in just three hours a day you *must* value the time you spend on your business. You'll be forced to evaluate each phone call, e-mail and distraction for it's time effectiveness. Show respect for your time and others will also respect your time.

Your business is now part of your lifestyle and intertwined with your family life. As a result you will think differently about work and you cannot afford to have an employee mentality now you are the Director. Be tough on yourself and don't tolerate unacceptable behaviour from yourself. You are only cheating yourself out of the success you deserve.

Ok, so you can't exactly fire yourself, and you don't have to endure annual appraisals so how are you going to ensure you perform and do a great job for your business?

MARK YOUR TERRITORY

You are going to need a dedicated workspace if you are running your business from home. Even if it's in a corner somewhere this space is your territory and needs to be marked as such. Put up photos, charts, planners, posters, quotes, messages and anything that will trigger positive, powerful and productive thoughts as you get to work. Don't get yourself stressed out too much if your territory gets messy when you are busy working on your business.

You don't have to be a super-tidy mummy to run a successful business. In fact I would suggest that you are going to need to tolerate some disorder because like family life a business can get chaotic at times so you need to be able to manage the chaos rather than create order. You will know that the state of your territory is affecting your productivity when you start to become frustrated by the mess, can't concentrate on tasks until your paperwork has been sorted and are unable to find a pen! It's not rocket science to work out some kind of system to keep your business files, correspondence, stationery, stock etc in order. Remember the objective of your time is to be productive and if you are spending too much time organising your business systems instead of getting and serving customers you are losing potential profits. Your time is always best spent growing your business because you can quickly and easily outsource support for your administration.

SHE'S IN A MEETING!

Set the boundaries from the start about how available you are. Of course when you are just starting out it's exciting to handle enquiries and be in demand. The problem starts when you use your productive time to answer the phone, return e-mails, and attend meetings, which take you away from actually working on your business. Being available right from the start can work for a while. *Always* being available will sabotage the growth of your business. Have a plan in place for how people can reach you and tell them what to expect from you.

For phone calls:

- Use a call minder service, receptionist or virtual assistant to take your calls.
- Voicemail – style your message to your brand/company/service and tell the caller when to expect a return call (same day? next business day)?
- Suggest the caller puts information or their request in an e-mail.

For e-mails:

- If you are asked to attend a meeting ask for the agenda to be sent in an e-mail first so you can be certain the meeting will be a productive use of your time.

- Send an automated reply to sender telling them when to expect a reply (by end of business day? within an hour?)
- It's tempting when you first start in business to become fixated on your inbox and it's exciting to see the messages coming in. You'll soon realise that sitting waiting for e-mails is an unproductive use of your time. If you are sitting next to your computer and it's not essential that you are online then just check your inbox on the hour, twice a day or whatever works for you.

LISTS FOR LISTS

You can't manage your time effectively if you feel overwhelmed and you just can't carry all you need to do around in your head. Get it out of your head and free your mind. You must make lists. Make as many lists as you need to keep on top of everything. Here are some examples:

- Diary – list your schedule each day for the year.
- To do list – Prioritised as high, medium and low.
- Call and e-mail list – priority list of all the people you need to call or e-mail.

Make your lists using whatever works best for you. A diary and year planner can work just as good as computer time management software.

Aim for completion not perfection!

BOOK YOURSELF UP

You want to block out as much time as possible in advance to minimise unproductive, unfocussed time. In your diary make sure you have blocked time for all the important activities connected with your business.

As a mumpreneur you'll also need to block time for all the important activities connected with your family. Enter holidays, activities and events that you want to attend as soon as they come in, then you'll avoid making business commitments that will clash and put you in the difficult position of having to choose. Even if you can only commit to half an hour slots of time because you are working from home with the children still make sure you block off that half an hour at a realistic time in the day when you'll have no distractions. Half an hour of productive time is worth more than an hour of unproductive time!

EVERY LITTLE HELPS

Waiting outside the school, stuck in traffic, feeding the baby, going for a walk in the park. 10 minutes here, 20 minutes there all adds up and you can take advantage of this loose time to learn. Most personal development, sales, marketing and business experts have audio products you can buy, so listening to a CD in the car, at home or on your MP3 player in the park is a great opportunity for you to educate yourself in business. Keep a notebook and pen handy at all times to jot down inspirational ideas you get for your business and solutions you come up with. Those aha moments won't stop coming so remember:

SUPERTIP

Don't just think it - ink it!

MUM POWER HOUR

This is no time for multi-tasking! Men are single focussed meaning that they pay attention to one thing at a time. Women have diffuse awareness, which gives us the ability to multi-task. There is a time to multi-task and a time to focus and the Mum Power hour must be your single focus time.

One of your biggest challenges when starting your business is making the time to focus on what needs to be done and taking action. Your business is going to go nowhere without implementation. Giving your business 100% focus is the only way to make progress. The good news is that you have already learned the difference between productive and non-productive time, so you know you need some regular focussed time to work through your plan.

I'm suggesting that you get into the habit of committing to a Mum Power Hour at least once a week. Even if you have no childcare or are still working full time it's possible to find a way to have just one hour a week to focus on your business. That doesn't mean you should spend this time giving your service, sending orders, making calls etc. This hour is like no other! Ideally these are the circumstances for your Mum Power Hour:-

- No distractions – no e-mail, no calls, no mobile, no Blackberry. If you work from home put a sign on the door or take yourself to another location like the library. You want to be in a position where you will get no interruptions.
- Decide what to focus on – Clearly define what needs your focus in this hour by saying, *"In the next hour I'm going to write my new marketing plan"* (for example).

- Surround yourself with resources – You may need your business materials, books, lists, mind maps and everything else you need to complete the task. Anything you don't have will cause you to break your focus while you think about this missing piece of information.
- Focus – launch into the task with complete focus. Although you have taken steps to avoid outside distractions there is still the potential for distraction within you. When your mind starts to wander you must snap back into focus and re engage yourself in the task.

SUPERTIP

Get lost! If they can't find you, they can't distract you.

WHY ARE YOU DOING IT ALL YOURSELF?

Starting your own business means you become the wearer of many hats and at first you are *everybody* in your business. When many people start up on their own they think that they must work alone too and insist on doing everything themselves – even the things they know they are no good at. They try in vain to keep their head above water but eventually their passion for their business becomes drowned in administration.

A consequence of you doing so well at implementing your plan is that your to-do list just gets bigger and bigger by the day. There is only so much you can do and your priority must be to use your strengths and analyse where your weaknesses lie. At some point as your business grows you are going to need support from other people to help you with your weak areas. That doesn't mean you have to start creating all kinds of jobs in your company (which is a quick way get through your profits).

The best way for you as a mumpreneur to get the right support, especially if you are based from home, is to outsource tasks to people who are skilled in that area. Heard of outsourcing? Outsourcing is not just for huge global organisations with call centres abroad. Successful people are outsourcing all over the country, and it's changing the face of enterprise.

In other words – delegate. You'll know when you are ready to delegate tasks because you will start to feel completely overwhelmed. Instead of enjoying working on your business you'll get a sick feeling of dread when you wake up when the reality of everything you have to get done hits you. The work just never seems to end and you seem to be in a strange virtual world where every spare minute is spent on the computer doing just one more thing, sending just another e-mail, looking at just another website. It wasn't supposed to be like this!

Well, it doesn't have to be like that! Success in business in the result of a team effort. Even if you are the only Director and get all the recognition when your business is doing well the truth is that you just can't get to the top by yourself. Accept that to grow your business you need to work with others who are strong where you are weak.

Outsourcing means that all those tasks that you have been struggling with can get done much quicker (and better) by someone who loves doing them! And what most mumpreneurs don't realise is this:

It's okay to pay someone else to do the things you aren't good at or you don't have any interest in.

When you hire outsourcers you'll have more time to focus on your most profitable activities. This is one of the biggest problems for any solo entrepreneur: their businesses aren't growing because they're simply not making enough time to grow them! They're so busy running their business that they're not working *on* their business. They're simply trying to do too much by themselves.

The sooner you see the benefits of outsourcing the better. You want to avoid getting yourself into a trap of trying to control every aspect of your business. If you think that nobody is capable of doing a job as good as you or that delegating will mean your standards will drop then you'll soon be in trouble. With the right people on board your standards can be doubled.

Mumpreneurs who have learned the secret of leveraging other people's time and expertise to help make them money are relaxed, calm and confident. They know that people and technology are busy 'running' the day-to-day business while they spend time doing what they do best.

One of the first people you might consider adding to your team is a Virtual Assistant. Virtual Assistants are freelancers who can do all your day-to-day running and administration tasks. They are independent and work on an "as required" basis from their own homes or offices. This saves you the hassle and expense of hiring a traditional office assistant. You might even find another mumpreneur buddy to work with you as many mums are working as VAs and setting up VA companies.

If you are concerned that your business can't afford to use a VA service the good news is that you don't have to hire a VA to work full time for you. A VA will only charge you for the hours worked and although their hourly rate is usually around £20-£30 you don't have the responsibility of employee conditions and benefits to worry about. You are paying for someone who enjoys what they do, already has all the necessary equipment and who will free up your time so you can work on marketing and growing your business.

3 GREAT REASONS TO USE A VA

1. They work on an as required basis from their own home or office.
2. Outsourcing tasks to them gives you more time to grow your business.
3. A VA will be more qualified and skilled in certain areas than you are and will do a quicker and better job.

WHAT A DIFFERENCE A VA MAKES!

Now you realise that there will be a time when you just can't live without a VA before you go rushing to appoint one take some time to think about what tasks you might want to delegate. Start to keep a log of all your daily and weekly tasks and do an 80/20 analysis to identify the top 20% most profitable tasks that you need to focus on or only you can do. The remaining 80% can start to be delegated. Here are some examples of such tasks:

- Responding to customer e-mails and phone calls
- Scheduling your appointments
- Internet research and fact-finding
- Maintaining your customer list
- Planning events
- Taking orders and sending orders
- Placing ads in publications and websites
- Creating PDF files and Powerpoint presentations
- Invoicing customers
- Sales Reports

- Liasing with your accountant to track expenses and keep up to date with tax records
- You might even want your VA to help you with personal tasks like researching the best mortgage and insurance deals or researching and booking your family holiday!

BUILD YOUR DREAM TEAM

You don't necessarily have to wait until you are at bursting point to get some support for your business. You can start building your dream team now to get support and the best advice so you can hit the ground running. If you are starting on a budget there are some low cost ways you can get help like hiring a student, an apprentice, retirees, stay at home mum friends or trading your product or service in exchange for someone's work.

Here are some ways for you to tap into resources that will help to transform your business:

Dream Team - Before Start Up	Dream Team - After Start Up
Mentors - authors of books, role models, networking contacts Coach - 1:1 or coaching program to work on implementation and strategies Volunteers - friends, family, partner, associates to help and support you Advisors - free advice about tax, accounts, grants etc	Mentors - keep learning Coach - keep you on track and get you there faster Volunteers - friends, family, partner, associates - help you with childcare, chores, projects and moral support Accountant - do you really need to spend time doing your own tax returns?

Web Coach/Designer - to advise you on web site development and strategies Suppliers - research how you can effectively work with any suppliers of goods or services	Web Coach/Designer - you need their expertise to maintain your website and implement new website strategies Virtual Assistants - help with the day to day admin and can now deal with any suppliers, orders and be your customer service department Project Manager - for when your business is growing rapidly and expanding with new products, services, campaigns and events PR Coach - to support you in getting exposure and recognition for your business

Now it's your turn. Here's an exercise to help you identify what support you need.

MY DREAM TEAM

Thinking about your business and the people you know, who could support you as you get your business off the ground and who could provide support as your business grows?

Dream Team - Before Start Up	Dream Team - Ongoing

KEY POINTS

- The difference between your business going nowhere and going places is *implementation*.

- So it's not about the *quantity* of time you have to spend on your business it's the *quality*.

- Deadlines work and you *must* create a habit of setting deadlines for yourself to work on your business.

- You have time and the time you have to work on your business must be the most focussed and productive of all.

- Be tough on yourself and don't tolerate. unacceptable behaviour from yourself. You are only cheating yourself out of the success you deserve.

- You don't have to be a super-tidy mummy to run a successful.

- Being available at the start works well but always being available will sabotage the growth of your business. Have a plan in place for how people can reach you and tell them what to expect from you.

- You want to block out as much time as possible in advance to minimise unproductive, unfocussed time.

- It's essential that you make focussed time to work through your plan.

- Get into the habit of committing to a Mum Power Hour at least once a week.

- The best way for you as a mumpreneur to get the right support, especially if you are based from home, is to outsource tasks to people who are skilled in that area.

- Mumpreneurs who have learned the secret of leveraging other people's time and expertise to help make them money are relaxed, calm and confident knowing that people and technology are busy 'running' the day to day business while they spend time doing what they do best.

The Marketing is More Important than the Mastery

"You cannot trust your own judgement. Test, test, test. Then test some more."

DAN KENNEDY

If you've already started your business maybe you've experienced *it*, if you're about to start maybe *it* hasn't hit you yet, maybe that's why you bought this book – because you know nothing about *it*. What is it? Marketing! It's the Mumpreneur Marketing Moment when after being carried away by the excitement of your idea and starting your business you realise you know absolutely nothing about marketing!

Here's the news – you'd better learn fast! You can easily get yourself up to speed with some really effective marketing strategies and because you are the sales and marketing department of your company it's important that you pay attention to marketing.

Right from the start the place where you should be directing your time, energy, creativity, common sense and resources is marketing. The only way for you to avoid being at the mercy of an expensive marketing consultancy is to personally master the sales and marketing aspects of your business. The breakthroughs in your business will come from your efforts in selling and marketing your business.

As I write the UK is experiencing the 'credit crunch' recession so it's more important than ever to focus on marketing. By the way – even in a recession businesses can still grow and thrive.

Marketing is one single skill you need to help your business grow while every-one around you is complaining that theirs is rotting! If you've got a hot market hungry for what you have to sell and you trigger the right emotional response that makes them want to buy and you have a sales process with a no risk guarantee – they'll buy.

Use different marketing strategies simultaneously and keep testing new ideas for their impact. After all marketing is just an experiment because you don't know for certain what the result will be or how much response you'll get. When you start your marketing strategy putting a tracking system in place will help you to find out what is working best. Something as easy as putting the question, *"How did you hear about us?"* in your materials is a simple way to start tracking.

You can take on more advanced tracking methods when you are up and running, just keep it in mind that you need to know how your customers are finding you so you can stop wasting any more time and money on ineffective strategies.

The great thing about marketing now that you are out there on your own and have no manager to approve of your ideas is that you can be interesting, fun and even outrageous with your marketing efforts. Who says you have to stick to the worn out, seen it-all-before, dull marketing ideas?

Here are some marketing strategies to get you started that can be implemented online and offline in your business. Some are simple, some are free and some require a little effort. The key is to not rely on just one.

MARKETING ALLIANCES

It's the biggest problem in any new business – how to get new customers. Most businesses start at a loss because part of the start up costs include the cost of 'buying' new customers through advertising etc.

Initially you are not making money from new customers because it'll take a while for you to recoup the cost of acquiring them. There's nothing actually wrong with this and many successful businesses start out this way.

There is a short cut to gaining new customers quickly by forming marketing alliances with other business owners whose customers are also your target customers.

The basis for a marketing alliance is when one business has the customers and the other business has something new to sell to them. Research websites and companies that sell complementary products or services to the same target market as yours. You simply work out a deal for the business owner, like a commission or one of your samples, in return for them promoting you to their customers. You must make it worthwhile and easy to get involved with you.

You can get this ready on your website by setting up an affiliate program through your shopping cart and setting the amount of commission you want to give an affiliate for each sale. You promote joining your affiliate program on your site and anyone who signs up for free to become an affiliate is given a unique link that they can use on their site to promote your business.

This is more than a simple link exchange because the website that send you visitors can make money from it. Because the affiliate has a unique number the shopping cart software can automatically track which affiliate website has sent you a visitor and if the visitor buys from you the affiliate is automatically paid the commission which you have set.

Okay so you won't be making as much on sales by making marketing alliances but you could save your-self time and money with not having to 'buy' customers through placing expensive adverts and you could get your business growing faster this way.

Here's an exercise to help you identify some possible marketing alliances for your business.

MY MARKETING ALLIANCES

Thinking of your business, list 3 possible marketing alliances you could form with other businesses that sell complementary products or services to your target market. Then think about the deal that you could offer each business to make it easy for them to promote your business to their customers.

Name of Business	Target Market	Products and/or Services	What's the Deal?

LEAD GENERATION ADS

If you can get enough new customers without paying for advertising – great! The reality is that most businesses need to place adverts to reach their target market.

Despite what the advertising salesperson tells you placing an advert for a set period isn't necessarily the most effective way to get customers. Most advertising follows the typical style of listing the company name, location, business hours, telephone number and e-mail address. Most advertisers never question whether this is effective because it's what everyone else is doing so it must work.

The problem is that you can't measure this kind of advertising. You just keep spending money on more ads without knowing if they are really giving you new customers. When spending your money on advertising be very choosy about where you advertise and make sure you are putting out lead generation ads asking for a direct response to the advert.

Which publications do your target market read? Which websites do they visit? Remember don't try to sell what you do, from the advert. The purpose of any advert you place is to get leads to visit your website and send or call for free information. Ask yourself, *"How will I know how many leads/customers I get from this ad?"*

Here's an exercise to help you plan where to place lead generation adverts.

WHERE IS MY TARGET MARKET?

Thinking about your target market list all the places where they might see a lead generation advert for your business. Here are some questions to help you.

1. Where do they go to regularly?
2. Which websites do they visit?
3. What magazines and newspapers do they read?

LOOK FOR COMPARABLES

If you feel stuck for marketing ideas or you feel your creativity has run dry look around for a comparable. This is another business selling a different and uncompetitive product or service but selling to your target market. Those comparable businesses share the same marketing challenges as you.

You could find some great ideas by seeing how they promote their business to your target market and could adapt some of the best ones to suit your business. For example a photographer specialising in family portraits might find interesting ways to promote their business by noticing how holiday companies sell to families, because both are about creating family memories, having fun, connecting family etc.

Prepare for finding ideas from other sources by getting yourself a 'swipe' file where you can store some of the best, attention grabbing stuff and you never have to feel stuck again!

MAKE YOUR E-MAIL SIGNATURE WORK FOR YOU

Most e-mail programs allow you to create your own signature block. Think about how many e-mails you send out – probably more than you think.

Make it easy for people to contact you from an e-mail instead of having to look up your number and if people want to put you in their contact management software (Outlook, Blackberry etc) they can simply copy and paste from your signature block.

Also e-mails get forwarded all the time so you never know where one of your e-mails might end up. Think of your signature block as a way to promote a new service, product or spread some news.

Here's a checklist of the info to include in your signature block – *not* all at once!

- Your name and title
- Your business name
- Your address
- Your business phone number
- Your fax number
- Your e-mail address
- Your web address
- Short phrase to describe your business or your strap line

Consider putting in some promotional info maybe as a P.S. like:

- An offer for a free sample
- An invitation to subscribe to your free newsletter
- An offer for a free trial
- A hyperlink to your latest promotion

Most e-mail software programs allow you to create several signatures so you can choose appropriate signatures for different businesses or promotions.

Here's an example:

```
=============================================
Ann Other Mumpreneur, Massage Therapist
http://www.massageU.com
Anytown's Premier Massage Service
mailto:Ann@massageU.com | Tel: 0844 666 9999
Sign up for free health and relaxation tips
=============================================
```

SURVEY YOUR PROSPECTS AND CUSTOMERS

Surveys aren't just for big corporations. You can easily create surveys to put on your website or send out in an e-mail to find out what your customers really want. This is an easy strategy yet not used enough. Find out what your customers want then give it to them!

If you are sending out your survey to prospects with only an e-mail contact you could get their postal address to use for a direct mail campaign in future. Take the opportunity to find out what publications they read, what websites they visit and how they found out about you by putting these questions in your survey to help you plan your marketing.

Offer a bonus for completing the survey and use the responses to guide you in making decisions about expanding your business.

I like *www.surveymonkey.com* for value and simplicity.

ASK FOR TESTIMONIALS

Testimonials are a really powerful marketing and selling tool and you must be proactive in asking for testimonials rather than waiting for them to come to you. Testimonials can be simply a couple of lines which you can use on your website and any promotional materials or they can be audio or video clips which are more effective.

This is no time for modesty and you'll probably find that your customers are more than happy to provide you with a testimonial. Just *ask*! Make sure you get permission to use their full name, company name and website address – don't use any other information like addresses or phone numbers. Make it fun for your customers to give you a testimonial, make them feel at ease with you and try to make it worth their while with a little something in return.

START AN E-ZINE

If you think you haven't got the time or haven't got enough to write to create a free e-zine – think again! An e-zine is simply a newsletter delivered by e-mail and it can be as simple as a few tips or can include tips, news, articles, offers and other resources.

You could get away with a simple text e-mail format but it looks boring compared to HTML format. HTML e-zines are read more often than text format, have higher click through rates and you can brand them with your logo, colours, images etc. You can buy e-zine publishing software from *www.aweber.com* and *www.constantcontact.com* for around £15 per month, that is simple to use and has the option of templates or you can create your own HTML style.

When it comes to content simply put yourself in the position of your reader. What would they find valuable and interesting? Include a snippet of personal information or share the latest developments in your business.

If you are comfortable with writing articles relating to your expertise then you must create short, informative articles for your e-zine. If you are not so comfortable then a little research will reveal a ton of information you could use in your newsletter just remember to always reference the source or give credit to the author. Take a look at *www.ezinearticles.com* for content ideas and if you are writing your own then submit them to this site and your article could end up being published in someone else's e-zine – anywhere in the world!

The bottom line is that publishing a regular e-zine is a great way for you to stay in touch with prospects and customers and sell more of your products and services.

An e-zine is the perfect way for you to establish yourself as an expert in your niche.

10 GREAT REASONS TO
START YOUR OWN E-ZINE

It doesn't matter whether you are selling a service or products a newsletter will:

1. Capture the e-mail addresses of your website visitors which gives you permission to contact them again and again.

2. Save money and time in printing and postage by producing your newsletter online instead of printing it.

3. Demonstrate to your current clients and prospects everything you have to offer them.

4. Build a loyal base of followers who are ready to work with you, buy from you and promote you to others.

5. Sell more services and products for you, online and offline.

6. Keep in touch with all of your customers and prospects on a regular basis.

7. Attract potential partners, endorsement requests, interviews, speaking invitations and other opportunities.

8. Be at the 'top-of-the-mind' of your clients and prospects. When they are ready and need or want your products or services, there's no question who they'll buy them from - you!

9. Effortlessly spread the word about your business. (Your newsletter can be the leverage you need to spread your message.)

10. Package what you know on a regular basis into tips and articles that can be reprinted in other publications for tons of additional exposure and traffic.

BLOGGING

A blog which is linked to your website is another great way for you to market your business and to get your prospects and customers to get to know, like and trust you. If you don't think your business needs a blog then think again. A blog is quick, free and easy to set up at *www.blogger.com* or *www.wordpress.com* and it can take as little as 5 minutes to add content to your blog.

Recycle articles. If you write a good article use it for your e-zine, your blog, submit it to www.ezinearticles.com, post it on your website and offer it to other publications.

Aim to publish new posts on your blog at least once a week to get you started and to keep it fresh and interesting – just put it on your to-do list! Then as you get more confident you can update it more often to build up to a regular routine.

Blogging is like writing a mini story and you'll be surprised by how much inspiration you'll find to write about. Don't worry about the standard of your writing. Keep sentences short. Like this. Think about what you are using your blog for – a business or a cause? Ideas might come to you from something that's happening in your business, an experience you've had, a trend that everyone is talking about, a trend that you want to start. Try to make your blog thought provoking *and* useful for the reader. Put your personality into your blog, give your readers a snapshot of what's happening in your life and ask questions to invite comments.

Pay special attention to your blog post headings because not only will people be drawn to the heading but search engines pick up on headings too which will help to drive more traffic to your site. Use powerful copy in your headlines as you would in your promotional copy to engage and encourage the reader to keep reading. Start reading and commenting on other people's blogs because a good blog is like a flowing conversation.

Warning: Your blog can be viewed by anyone, anywhere and anything that you say in your blog could be used against you. Avoid getting into arguments with people with strong opinions and getting personal, and be careful of libel. If you say something about a person that is untrue in a blog it's libellous and could expose you to legal action. Just use your common sense when blogging!

Here are some great reasons to be a blogger.

5 WAYS TO BLOG

1. Marketing – talk about new launches, developments, plans and include a link to your website.
2. Get known – engage your readers, prospects and customers with some personal information and help them to get to know, like and trust you.
3. Be an expert – use your blog to share your expertise.
4. Market research – asking questions in a blog is a very good way of engaging readers and getting them to comment. People love to see their name in print and allowing them to comment on your blogs makes it easy for them to do so.
5. Lobbying – your business may need help from others to ensure your survival or to fight a cause. Your blog could help you to get support and gather evidence.

SUPERTIP

You can set up a blog before you set up your website; start promoting your up-and-coming website, invite comments and make links with other bloggers who could support you.

NETWORKING

Being a mumpreneur working from home is a lonely job if you have no network to support you. Meeting other people in business will give you a boost and will give you a new sense of belonging. I recommend that you also purposefully seek out a new peer group of like-minded people who you can network with and you could even make some great new friends.

If you are feeling nervous about getting out there to network you're just going to have to get over it! The harsh reality is that to be a success you just can't do it alone – even though it may seem like you have to others. All successful business people have a team of people or employees to support them and have built up contacts, business associates and advisors and relationships with other successful people. It's the combination of all this mixed with the desire to succeed that really makes a person successful in business.

Experiment with networking mainly to get exposure for yourself and your business but to also share ideas and get feedback. Some networking meetings are very structured and work on a sales approach. Others are more casual and are about making contacts and sharing information. A good way to get yourself into a relaxed state in networking situations is to focus on the person you are engaging with and be curious by asking them questions about themselves and their business. Allowing the other person to tell you about their business might make it easier to then turn the conversation to focus on you.

When you start your business you'll have more time than money and time spent networking could be a great investment. Don't be disheartened if you don't get instant results. Think about networking like planting a seed that over time will grow. It's important that you get out there and meet people who might be interested in your business. It will also help you to practice talking about your business with passion and conviction.

There are many websites that could help you to network online in forums. First check what the policy is concerning promoting your business as some discussion forums don't allow blatant self-promotion. If that's the case you can still take part in the discussion by offering your advice or opinion.

SOCIAL MEDIA

Social media like Facebook, MySpace and Twitter are all free to join and are great as a marketing and networking tool. It's so easy to set yourself up with a profile about you and your business and you can start connecting with people in minutes.

Don't assume that using social media will bring you sales directly from customers though. It's more realistic to use it as a way to 'meet' people and get to know them before marketing to them or trying to pitch them.

Give people an understanding of the essence of your business and you by posting messages through social media. As a mum working from home social media can connect you with 'friends' worldwide with whom you could share ideas, learn from, form alliances or simply enjoy keeping in touch.

SUPERTIP

Join Facebook for free at www.facebook.com Search for me and send me a friend request. I'll be your first Facebook friend!

KEY POINTS

- Right from the start the place where you should be directing your time, energy, creativity, common sense and resources is marketing.
- There is a short cut to gaining new customers quickly by forming marketing alliances with other business owners whose customers are also your target customers.
- When spending your money on advertising be very choosy about where you advertise and make sure you are putting out lead generation ads asking for a direct response.
- Make it easy for people to contact you from an e-mail instead of looking up your number. Think of your signature block as a way to promote a new service, product or spread some news.
- You can easily create surveys to put on your website or send out in an e-mail to find out what your customers really want.
- Publishing a regular e-zine is a great way for you to stay in touch with prospects and customers and sell more of your products and services.

- Like an e-zine a blog which is linked to your website is another great way for you to market your business and to get your prospects and customers to get to know, like and trust you.
- Experiment with networking mainly to get exposure for yourself and your business, but to also share ideas and get feedback.
- Social media like Facebook are great for networking and sharing information.

How to Create a Website that Gets Customers & Makes Money

"Adults are always asking kids what they want to be when they grow up because they are looking for ideas."

PAULA POUNDSTONE

The Internet, what would we do without it? For a mumpreneur going online with her business is liberating and I don't know yet of any business that would not benefit from being out there on the worldwide web. Increasingly people are using the Internet as their primary source for gaining information. You name it – it's on the net!

The fact is though that the majority of people are looking for information online – not to buy things. This is great for mums wanting to start a business because taking advantage of technology has transformed many of the traditional problems of setting up a business (like leasing premises and hiring staff) into a golden opportunity to go global from your kitchen table! Your website is the location of your business and is 'open' 24/7. People can come and browse from anywhere in the world, day and night so you want to be sure you have something to entice them with when they arrive!

There is a downside to the huge popularity of the Internet: thanks to all the rubbish out there people are generally becoming more choosey about which websites they will buy from.

Spend some time now thinking about what your website is supposed to do. You might think it's obvious but actually many website owners are not clear about what they expect their website to do for their business. Be realistic with your expectations at the start because the chances of a visitor stumbling upon your site and whipping their credit card out instantly to buy loads of stuff are close to zero.

When a visitor comes to your site you need to have a strategy in place to make sure you make an impact and get a response. You could collect names and e-mail addresses by offering some free information like tips, an e-zine or latest special offers.

If visitors to your site have never met you in person before or are not previous customers you also need to have a strategy in place for building trust and potentially a relationship with them.

Don't be fooled into thinking that just because you have a website your business will work like magic. The majority of visitors to your site will not do business with you. The Internet is just one way that you are promoting your business and is the place where you direct people to find out more. You still need to have a strategy and process in place to turn website visitors into customers. Once you have got this in place and it's working effectively with adequate traffic it can be like magic! Think of your website as a way to generate leads because it's going to be much easier for you to sell to people who are interested in your business and have given you their contact details.

DON'T HIRE A WEB DESIGNER YET!

You don't have to be a 'geek' to run your business online. If you have expert IT skills and are comfortable with designing and maintaining your own site that's great. If, like me, you can just about send an e-mail and write a word document that's great too! Thanks to fantastic software like Xsite Pro, Joomla and Microsoft Front Page you can even create your own website. I have used Xsite Pro to create a new style for my website and found it simple and great value too. It's easier than you think to create a website from scratch and even a complete novice could design their own custom web pages and publish them on the web.

Xsite Pro in particular comes with a feature that makes it simple for you to add a sign up option with an autoresponder to your pages and link to PayPal so you can start taking orders as soon as you are online.

To attract leads your website needs to be easy to understand, interesting and to engage visitors – make it *sticky*. The key to a sticky website is good content and powerful copy. Give your visitors reasons to stick around.

To get your business online and ready to make you money you'll need:

- A domain name and hosting
- A website – hire a web designer or create your own
- An autoresponder – to keep your list of e-mail addresses collected and to send automatic responses
- A product or service
- A merchant account for example PayPal or WorldPay
- Shopping cart software – more options for automation

If you're not sure about creating your own web pages and would prefer to hire a web designer I recommend that you ask for a website with a CMS - content management system. This means that after the site has been created you will be able to make any changes or additions to the content on your website yourself and won't have to keep asking (and paying!) your web designer. Having a CMS makes it possible for you and a web designer to collaborate on your website and gives you more control over your online presence.

SUPERTIP

Don't try to send broadcast e-mail messages through your own everyday e-mail program. Most reliable Internet service providers will think you are a spammer and you could get blocked.

GET THEM ON YOUR LIST

When people visit your website you need to have a strategy in place to capture contact information. The easiest is just to collect a name and e-mail address as you may find more resistance if you ask for postal addresses and phone numbers at this stage. Remember the majority of your website visitors are browsing not buying.

Imagine that your website is actually a shop and your visitor is a customer. When they come into your shop they might experience any one of these scenarios:

- You ask them if you can help them to which they reply, "No thanks just looking", then browse for a while and leave.
- You acknowledge them but you are busy and unable to serve them so they browse and leave.
- You ignore them because you are chatting with a friend so they leave without even browsing!
- They tell you exactly what they are looking for and you sell it to them then they leave.

Notice that in every scenario the customer leaves and you have no way of attracting them back into your shop. If they do come back, it's probably by chance. Even when a customer has bought something if you have no way of contacting them again you are losing out on potential sales. It's so much easier and more cost effective to sell your products and services to people who have bought from you already. Having put so much time and effort into choosing your target market and getting ready to sell your product or service the key to your profitability is to build a list of people interested in your business – your *prospects*. Once you start your lead generation process sooner or later people will start visiting your site. As soon as they arrive they will arrive at your *landing page* and there must be a way for you to grab their attention and get them to do something – to opt-in or sign-up.

Here are some responses that you might want from your website visitors:

- Sign up for some free information providing a name and e-mail address
- Fill out a profile
- Complete a survey
- Submit a questionnaire
- Join your organisation

Offering something of real value for free will get the best response in terms of numbers, however bear in mind that there are some people who will be happy to get the free information from you but never actually buy. Offering something for a low cost will give you more qualified leads because they have invested some money already to get your information.

If you're unsure which approach to go for don't worry because you can always test each one to see which gives you the best response. There's a saying that goes, *"The best word to use in marketing is free!"* If the copy on your website is so compelling that after reading it your visitors think, *"This is for me"*, then make it easy for them to get some free information from you. In marketing this is called the *'most wanted response'* or MWR. Think about websites that you have visited and start looking at home/landing pages more closely now and see for yourself the different most wanted responses. Avoid the traditional methods such as:

"Call now for a free consultation"

"Call for more details"

"Contact us for a brochure"

Why? Because you are leaving it up to the visitor to make the next move. It's more of an effort for them to have to pick up the phone to call you or fill out a form to get a brochure sent. People are busy – they want it *now*. After they have left your site and go back to their busy lives their attention will be instantly diverted elsewhere and calling you could be the last thing on their mind. Make it as quick and easy as possible for your visitors to fill in a box with their name and e-mail address – *to sign up*. One click and you have generated a lead that came to your site 'cold' but is now on your list of 'warm' prospects.

Your prospects are your future 'hot' customers so you must make sure that you look after them and fulfil your promise of free information. There are so many creative ways that you could provide your freebie. Depending on how much time you have you can create a PDF containing a special report, tips, mistakes to avoid, secrets etc which can be accessed instantly when your prospect signs up. Or you can offer a free e-mail newsletter – an *e-zine*. E-zines are a great and creative way to keep in touch with your list so e-zine strategies will be covered in more detail in the marketing chapter. No matter what kind of business you are in you can always provide information of interest.

Remember people have come to your site because they are interested in the solution you provide. Put yourself in the shoes of a visitor arriving at your website – what kind of free information would entice you? Don't make your freebie compete for attention with too much clutter on your home page. Think carefully about how many options there are on your home page and keep it as simple as possible, making it loud and clear what you are leading the reader to do – sign up for your freebie?

SUPERTIP

Whether it's the name of your e-zine or your free report the title needs to grab attention. The best position for your freebie offer and most wanted response is in the upper right hand side of the page because the eye is naturally drawn to the right hand side of any page.

ATTENTION GRABBING TITLES FOR FREEBIES

Here are some examples of titles for your freebie:

"The 10 Biggest Mistakes Made by..."

"How to...in 7simple steps"

"3 Simple Ways to..."

"The 5 simple secrets to..."

"Why you must..."

"Everything you need to know about..."

Now it's your turn to create your freebie. Here's an exercise to help you:

MY FREEBIE

1. Thinking of your target market, what kind of information would they find the most useful?

2. Thinking of your time commitments, what kind of format would be most realistic? Bearing in mind you need to contact your prospects regularly what could you commit to? For example free tips: daily or weekly? E-zine: weekly or monthly? Special offers and announcements: weekly, monthly, seasonal?

3. Thinking of the content, what kind of title could you give your e-zine, special report, article etc? Come up with at least 3 different ideas.

After they have signed up and received your freebie don't neglect them. Your list is a bank of prospects who could easily become customers in the future. You need to have a strategy in place for a follow up process that allows you to continue contacting your prospects. This is known as *multi-step marketing*. This could be sending a sales letter, making a phone call, sending an e-mail or sending an e-zine. Apparently marketing messages need to be repeated around 7 – 9 times before a person decides to buy. The fortune is in the follow up.

GENERATING LEADS

Take a look at the website *www.alexa.com* to see how much traffic other websites are getting. Your objective is to expose your business to your target market and give them compelling reasons to go and visit your website.

The traditional way to promote a business is to place an ad somewhere that simply says what your product or service does. People see your ad and they either buy or they don't buy. There is no way to communicate with the majority of potential customers who might be interested but for various reasons don't buy as soon as they see your ad.

A much more effective way to promote your business is to generate leads – or lead generation. The process of lead generation helps you to separate the potential buyers in your target market from the others who are not interested. Most lead generation starts with an ad encouraging people to contact you for more information or in this case to visit your website for information.

Your promotion must contain compelling reasons for your target market to respond and the best way is to tell them what problem you solve. Don't try to make a sale from your lead generation advert – so no mention of costs, special offers etc. The purpose of any lead generation is to get people who are interested in your product or service to take some kind of action and this is where your freebie comes in. You're simply weeding out those people who are in your target market but aren't interested in learning more about your product or service. For example this is one of the ways I generate leads to *www.supermummy.com*:

MARKETING FOR MUMPRENEURS MADE EASY!

At last! A simple and practical online coaching and marketing service exclusively for mumpreneurs – helping you to grow your business and yourself.

To sign up for a FREE Supermummy Success e-zine and BONUS report visit www.supermummy.com

---

Notice that there is no hard selling going on here, no persuading someone to buy something they don't really want or have a need for.

Most website visitors will just browse around a site when they visit for the first time, even if they saw your lead generation ad. Note again that with this kind of lead generation advertising you are aiming to build a list of quality leads who are interested in your product or service and are willing to give you their contact information for some free information.

Now it's your turn. Here's an exercise to help you create your own lead generation advert.

MY LEAD GENERATION AD

1. Create a headline to which includes who your product/service is for is for and at least one benefit
2. Briefly say what problem your product or service solves and include more benefits
3. Tell them what your offer is and where to go to get it
4. Now put it all together and create your complete advert with headline, problem solver, benefits, offer and where to go

It's so much easier and better for you to drive people to your website and offer something for free than to drive them directly to a sale. Instead of chasing a sale you are attracting potential customers and by signing up for some tips, an e-zine or special offers they are giving you permission to contact them regularly.

Here are some ways that you can find your leads both online and offline. Most successful websites use a combination of lead generation strategies so don't think you have to choose only one or two. If you don't understand some of the terminology – all will be explained later in the chapter.

HOW TO FIND YOUR LEADS

Online	Offline
Through search engine listings	Getting articles published in magazines & newspapers
Pay Per Click Ads	
Getting articles published on websites	Featuring in a magazine or newspaper
Getting articles published in e-zines	Networking
	Through word of mouth
Through discussion forums	Doing radio/tv interviews
Through blogs	Being a guest speaker
Through links from other websites	Offering your own seminar
	Attending shows and events
Advertising on websites or in e-zines	Direct mail letter
Networking	Advertising in publications

UNDERSTANDING SEARCH ENGINES

Not all of your website visitors will be there because they saw your lead generation advert. Remember most people are browsing the Internet looking for information and the number one way that people find websites is by using a search engine.

Why not get your website right in front of the people who are actually searching for your product or service? Search engines can be a consistent source of your visitors – your *traffic*. The way that people use search engines is by using *keywords* for example, keywords to find the Supermummy website could be:

"Working from home"

"Mumpreneur"

"Online business"

To find out exactly how many people are searching for particular keywords and phrases that might apply to your business use *www.wordtracker.com.*

All search engines use keywords as an indicator of how high to rank your website in the search results. The keywords you use on your website should also drive the keywords you use elsewhere online such as Pay Per Click, articles, blogs etc. There is actually a lot to learn about how you can get your site ranked as high as possible and not being a 'geek' I can only give you the basics here. With the search engine optimisation rules changing all the time I recommend you seek assistance from an expert.

Pay Per Click advertising like Google AdWords means that you can get your website listed higher in the results search by creating an advert. You select which keywords are specific to your business and if any of those keywords are searched for your advert will be displayed in the results. You only pay if someone clicks on your advert to go through to your website. You can set a daily, weekly or monthly limits on the amount you want to be charged. The advantage with PPC is that you can have a lead generation advert that will be displayed when a potential customer is searching for keywords related to your product or service.

SUPERTIP

Fancy graphics and a Flash introduction
don't sell. Powerful words sell.

SEARCH ENGINE OPTIMISATION AND PAY PER CLICK COMPARISON

SEO (usually on left hand side of screen)	PPC (usually top or/ right hand side)
Free listings based on relevance to keywords	Paid listings based on relevance to keywords, price and click through rate
Long term - do some SEO work on your site to consistently get listed higher	Short term - gets you traffic quickly
Can spend too much time on SEO	Quick and easy to set up
Information shown may not relate specifically to the keywords selected	Better for lead generation because you create an ad

3 PHASES OF A WEBSITE CAMPAIGN

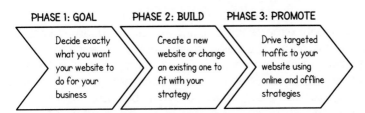

PHASE 1: GOAL

Decide exactly what you want your website to do for your business

PHASE 2: BUILD

Create a new website or change an existing one to fit with your strategy

PHASE 3: PROMOTE

Drive targeted traffic to your website using online and offline strategies

A WEBSITE MARKETING AND INCOME GENERATING STRATEGY

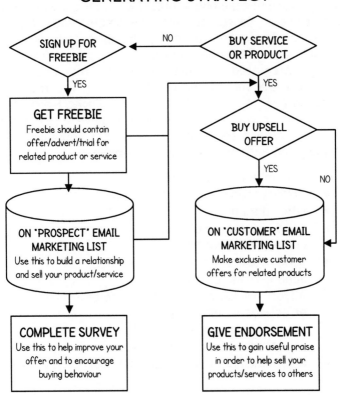

SIGN UP FOR FREEBIE

NO

BUY SERVICE OR PRODUCT

YES

YES

GET FREEBIE
Freebie should contain offer/advert/trial for related product or service

BUY UPSELL OFFER

YES

NO

ON "PROSPECT" EMAIL MARKETING LIST
Use this to build a relationship and sell your product/service

ON "CUSTOMER" EMAIL MARKETING LIST
Make exclusive customer offers for related products

COMPLETE SURVEY
Use this to help improve your offer and to encourage buying behaviour

GIVE ENDORSEMENT
Use this to gain useful praise in order to help sell your products/services to others

A SHOPPING CART THAT
MAKES YOU MONEY!

If your only experience of using an online shopping cart is as a customer then you might not be aware of how fantastic this software is for a mumpreneur with an online business. Shopping cart software gives you the ability to *automate* much of your business which will makes life so much easier for you. This is when you let technology do the work for you.

You and/or your web designer can set up your shopping cart software to take online orders automatically and also contact your prospects and customers with e-mail marketing. There are too many shopping cart software providers to mention here but you'll need a professional package integrated with marketing tools that cost from around £60 per month and usually offer a free trial. To learn more I recommend *www.1shoppingcart.com* but maybe you or your web designer will have a preferred choice. Here are some of the ways that shopping cart software can automate your business online:

- Sell unlimited products
- Collect credit and debit card payments
- Offer discounts
- Keep a database of your prospects and customers – your list
- Send broadcast e-mails to your list
- Send e-zines to your list
- Advert tracker and split tests – to test effectiveness of ads
- Automatic response to people who sign up for your freebie – *autoresponders*
- Automatic downloads of digital products and e-books

It's not essential to have shopping cart software to start because for example with Xsite Pro software you can set up a website that links to an autoresponder and directly to PayPal to process online credit/debit card payments. Whether you need a shopping cart or not will depend on what you are offering through your website.

CONVERSIONS

After you have started generating leads and have traffic coming to your site you'll need to start measuring the number of people signing up compared to the total number of visitors – your *conversion rate*. There are various ways this can be done for free such as through *www.webstat.com* or Google Analytics. For example if 1000 visitors come to your site and 50 sign up for your freebie and join your list then you have a conversion rate of 5%. This is actually really good! It's common for a website to get a conversion rate of 3-4% at first.

Remember that the majority of people are online looking for *information* not to buy. Even if someone has responded to your lead generation ad and has visited your site the majority will still be 'just looking' at first. You might be thinking that it's a miracle you get any conversions at all! Now you understand what it really takes to actually get a website visitor onto your list hopefully you also understand why it's so important to take care of them.

So now you have two ways to increase the number of your conversions:

1. Increase future traffic to your site
2. Test different strategies of converting current visitors into prospects

I use the word 'test' because marketing is all just a big experiment and you won't know for certain if your site is working as effectively as it could be. Making some small adjustments could dramatically affect what your visitors do. Don't worry too much about it at first just get your website online and start getting some traffic.

Bear in mind though that raising traffic alone is not the only answer to getting more conversions. Think about some of the reasons why the visitors who have already come to your site may not have decided to sign up to your list. It's all a continuous process of testing to see what works well and what doesn't work so well.

Keep your site fresh with updates, new offers, product launches, and special announcements to give your visitors a reason to come back. Ultimately your website is going to be a work in progress. It's not going to be perfect and there will always be something that needs to be tweaked. The beauty about having a website as the 'location' of your business is that you can be creative and try out new ideas and improve it as you grow your business.

So now you've got your lead generation strategies sending interested visitors to your site and you're confident that you have a great freebie offer to get them on your list what next? There's no point going to all this effort to build a list of potential customers if you're not going to use it effectively. You have a list of names and e-mail addresses that can be sent useful information via e-mail but be careful not to abuse it by constantly sending them useless stuff.

The best way to proceed with a list of prospects is to have a plan to contact them regularly to market your business – *multi-step marketing*. To implement multi-step marketing you are going to need some marketing strategies. To maximise sales you are going to need some sales strategies. It's all coming in the next few chapters but first I want to share with you one of the most profitable ways to generate an automated online income.

KEY POINTS

- The majority of people are looking for information online – not to buy things.
- Think of your website as a way to generate leads because it's going to be much easier for you to sell to people who are interested in your business and have given you their contact details.
- You can create your own website with software like Xsite Pro or collaborate with a web designer using a CMS – content management system.
- To attract leads your website needs to be easy to understand, interesting and to engage visitors – make it *sticky*. The key to a sticky website is good content and powerful copy.
- The purpose of any lead generation is to get people who are interested in your product or service to take some kind of action.
- Most successful websites use a combination of lead generation strategies so don't think you have to choose only one or two.
- Search engines can be a consistent source of visitors – your traffic. The way that people use search engines is by using *keywords*.
- Pay Per Click advertising like Google AdWords means that you can get your website listed higher in the results search by creating an advert.
- Once you start your lead generation process sooner or later prospects will start visiting your site. As soon as they arrive they will arrive at your *landing page* and there must be a way for you to grab their attention and do something – to opt-in.

- One click and you have generated a lead that came to your site 'cold' but is now on your list of 'warm' prospects. Your prospects are your future 'hot' customers so you must make sure that you look after them and fulfil your promise of free information.
- No matter what kind of business you are in you can provide information of interest. Remember people have come to your site because they are interested in the solution you provide and you are the expert in your business.
- You need to have a strategy in place for a follow up process that allows you to continue contacting your prospects – which is known as *multi-step marketing*. This could be sending a sales letter, making a phone call, sending an e-mail or sending an e-zine.
- To succeed online you may need shopping cart software to *automate* your business which will makes life so much easier for you. This is when you let technology do the work for you.
- After you have started generating leads and getting traffic to your site you'll need to measure the number of people signing up compared to the total number of visitors – your *conversion rate*.
- You can increase the number of conversions by increasing the number of visitors or making your site more effective at converting prospects into customers.

How to Make Money While You Sleep with Information Marketing

*"T'Aint What You Do
(It's The Way That You Do It)."*

MELVIN OLIVER AND JAMES YOUNG

Now you're aware that most internet searches are for information you may still be blissfully unaware of how you can take advantage of this huge demand by taking the opportunity to provide information – at a cost. Thanks to our 'now' society and increasing pressure on people's time you can sell your knowledge, expertise and experience to give people a shortcut.

Are some of those millions of people using the internet willing to pay for information? Yes! By leveraging the best of what you know you can package information for your target market into either digitally delivered products or hard copy products and sell and deliver them through your website – this is called *information marketing*. By selling information which could be bought at any time of the day or night, from any country, you could generate additional income and literally make money while you sleep!

Here are some really big advantages to information marketing:

- Work anywhere from a computer – the computer software handles the sales and orders
- No staff required
- Low start up costs
- Large profit margin

- Replaces 1:1 with 1:many - you are able to 'multiply yourself'
- Passive income

So how do you make money from information? You don't need to be the world expert in general knowledge to create and sell an information product. You just need to know something that others want to know and be able to market that information. The key factor to success is having prospects who are hungry for information. Understand what it is that your market wants and create information products that satisfy them. You will establish an expert position with your customers and will stand out from the competition that may not be as enterprising.

9 GREAT REASONS TO SELL INFORMATION PRODUCTS

1. Information products (digital e-books, e-courses, audio programs, home study courses) - all have very low production costs. If you can send an e-mail and write a word document you can create an information product.

2. Your products can be printed or produced on demand eliminating the need for stock and storage.

3. The Internet market continues to grow rapidly and people worldwide will always be looking for information. Your information product could be purchased from anywhere with just a few clicks.

4. All you need is an Internet connection and you are connected to your office and your customers. Having income from information products means you can be completely mobile with your business.

5. Passive income generation systems (after you have produced your products and worked out a

marketing and sales system) can allow automation to take over while you take a break.

6. Information products can bridge the gap between a free consultation and a sale. If you provide a service and have nothing else to offer you could be missing out on additional income because some customers may not be 'ready' to buy your complete service but might be happy to buy some information relating to your service.

7. You can have different income streams coming into your business by creating some information products.

8. Packaging your knowledge into information products gives your prospects a chance to sample your business at a lower cost before committing to your high cost offers.

9. You can use your information products as a marketing tool by sending copies with your press releases, using them in lead generation ads or having copies available at events.

HOW TO CREATE AN E-BOOK IN 7 SIMPLE STEPS

If you can write a word document or record yourself speaking you can create an information product. You need to share the best of what you know about a topic with people who are interested in it. Here's an example of how to create an e-book:

1. Open a word document and create a cover page that could include your book title, author name, business logo, a photo or graphic, a brief description.

2. About the author – tell your story, promote the benefits of your product or service.

3. Table Of Contents – use the automatic feature in Word.

4. The Content – Chapters – Step by step instructions, using powerful and easy to read copy.
5. Include an upsell to your product or service.
6. Add a disclaimer to avoid legal issues.
7. Convert to a PDF – with adobe acrobat software or free software on the Internet.

That's it! You have an e-book which you can use for your freebie as a digital download, you can use it as a bonus for sales, you can make a small charge for it to gain highly qualified prospects and you can print it out and take it to events.

Once you have your e-book ready you can move on to more varied products like recording an audio onto CD and could package them together. Start with one product that is easiest for you and work up from there.

Step 4 is the most daunting part. But don't underestimate just how much you know and the expertise you have. This is no time for modesty. If you have special knowledge that others could really benefit from why not be creative about how you share that information? In fact offering information products in addition to your regular product or service might be just another reason to make you stand out. Compared to your competition that only offer their one product or service you can establish your-self as the expert and gain more credibility.

Now it's your turn. Here's an exercise to help you create an information product.

MY INFORMATION PRODUCT

1. Thinking of your product or service what kind of information product could you create first?

2. What special knowledge, expertise and information could you share in your product?

3. What problem can you help to solve with your information?

What would you think if your regular salon were to send you an e-zine packed with top tips and special offers or if you enquired about a mortgage and received a really useful guide and regular updates on changes in the financial system? How might it affect you? Would you be more impressed? Would you be more likely to become a customer or remain a loyal customer if you received regular attention?

By putting a system in place in your business of offering free information and following up regularly you are keeping your business in the mind of your current or potential customers. Even if someone isn't ready to buy from you yet following up automatically means when they are ready to buy they think of you. This might make more sense to you if I give you some examples of how information products could be used in a business.

Here some examples of how information products could be used in different types of businesses.

Health and Beauty	Financial Services	Events
Website with freebie of weekly e-zine - tops tips, advice etc	Website with freebie of e-book - How to…, The truth about…	Website with freebie of Special Report - Checklist for planning an event
E-book - How to…	More e-books covering different areas of finance	E-book - Event Planning Secrets Revealed
Secrets to…	Audio CD - Take Control of Your Finances in 7 Steps	Special Announcements by e-mail sharing testimonials and news from other events
Special Report - Get Fit Now… How to look Good at 50…	Upsell with a Personal Financial Makeover 1:1 consultation	Teleseminar sharing the key facts about what makes a great event and offer your services at the end
Home study course - expert advice and strategies with 1:1 consultation included		

THE MUMPRENEUR MARKETING FUNNEL

Another way to help you understand this concept is to think of your business in the shape of a funnel.

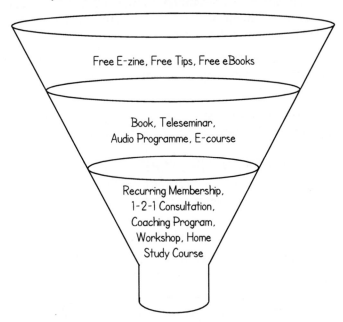

Free E-zine, Free Tips, Free eBooks

Book, Teleseminar, Audio Programme, E-course

Recurring Membership, 1-2-1 Consultation, Coaching Program, Workshop, Home Study Course

The top of the funnel is the widest part and this allows for the majority of leads coming into your business and signing up for your freebie. Your leads are now prospects and more likely to buy further products and services – if you have something else to offer them!

Information products that you could have in the middle of your funnel might be a workbook, a guide, a teleseminar, a CD audio seminar and an e-course. The objective is to move your customers down to the bottom of the funnel where you sell your highest cost product or service. It's easier for you to sell these to customers that have already bought from you and sampled your expertise.

The bottom of your funnel is where your top 20% of customers will be – the ones that have bought from you previously and are continuing to buy at a higher cost. Give them recognition and thanks by paying special attention to your best customers.

Ideas for the bottom of your funnel could be a private consultation, a coaching program, a workshop and best quality product.

Now it's your turn to create your own Mumpreneur Marketing Funnel for your business. Here's an exercise to help you.

MY MUMPRENEUR MARKETING FUNNEL

1. What information products could you offer for free to generate leads?

2. What could you offer in the middle for variety and additional income?

3. What are your best and highest priced products and services for the bottom?

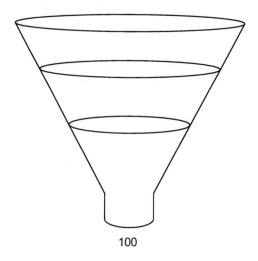

KEY POINTS

- Leverage the best of what you know. You can package information for your target market into either digitally delivered products or hard copy products and sell and deliver them through your website.

- The key factor to success is having customers who are hungry for information. Understand what it is that your market wants and create information products which gives them what they want.

- Information products can be digital e-books, e-courses, audio programs, home study courses – all have very low production costs. If you can send an e-mail and write a word document you can create an information product.

- You can have different income streams coming into your business by creating some information products.

- Packaging your knowledge into information products gives your prospects a chance to sample your business at a lower cost before committing to your high cost offers.

- If you have special knowledge that others could really benefit from why not be creative about how you share that information? In fact offering information products in addition to your regular product or service might be just another reason to make you stand out.

Sales Mum

"Start Where You Are. Use What You Have. Do What You Can."

ARTHUR ASHE

Why does the thought of selling fill people with dread? Why do we sometimes associate selling with pressure and manipulation? Why do we like to talk about our experiences of pushy salespeople and seem to forget the helpful ones?

We've all been there as a customer trying to beat the salesperson at their game by fobbing them off with "I can't afford it", "I need to think about it" or "Send me some information". It's understandable when someone is trying to sell you something that you haven't enquired about, have shown no interest in or have absolutely no need for.

But what about the times when you have really *wanted* to buy something? Maybe you've sent off for some details, perhaps you've already decided on the exact model you want or you really need somebody's expert help and are willing to pay whatever the price even before the salesperson has opened their mouth! The truth is that everyone likes to buy and nobody wants to be sold to!

With all sales there is a critical *motivating factor* that makes people buy and to make a sale you need to find out or work out what that is for your customer. Motivating factors are the emotions that someone has connected with buying the product or service.

For example people have different motivating factors for buying a car. Some might buy a particular model because of the status it gives them yet others might buy the same car because of the security and peace of mind gained from its safety features. You'll learn more about how to stir up emotions later in this chapter but for now think about how this relates to the target market selection process you have been through.

If you've chosen a target market of people with a real need for a product or service and you've come up with the solution then selling it to them is going to be easier for you. Aim to be seen as a problem solver rather than a salesperson.

When you are discussing your product or service with a potential customer be friendly and ask questions to find out if they really are a match and help them to understand that you have exactly what they want. Take some time to build rapport and avoid trying to sell as soon as the discussion starts. You want your customers to feel like you respect them and have their best interests at heart – which you do! By asking the right questions you can give the best advice and being perceived as an advisor or expert will help you to build some trust with potential customers.

Another great way for you to be successful in selling is to make people feel like they are being taught about your product or service. Being educated about how something will benefit them will generate much less resistance than being told and sold.

One of the keys to your success will be gaining repeat business. Don't think of any customer as a one off sale like a one night stand. It's a waste of your time and money to constantly find new customers. The best strategy is to have satisfied customers stay with you to enjoy a long and meaningful relationship!

As your website will be a salesperson on your behalf keep in mind that first time visitors to your site may not know you, like you or trust you yet and all they see is that you have a product or service to sell to them. It's sad but true that some people will be cynical and will look for reasons to see the worst in what you are offering. Feelings of doubt, resistance and possibly fear can be associated with buying online. The Internet is not a place for impulse buying! Because you are not there in person to greet your visitors, ask questions and assist them you need to sell yourself and the benefits of your product or service with short, clear and precise words that communicate your message *and* answer their questions– *your copy*.

MAKE YOUR SALES PAGE
DO THE SELLING FOR YOU

Powerful and influential copy is your secret weapon when it comes to promoting your business. Think about all the successful products and services you know – what do they all have in common? Memorable and compelling copy.

Copywriting is one of the most valuable skills in marketing. Many professionals make a killing doing it 9-5. Why? Because when it's done well copy alone has the power to make money for any business.

Copywriting is writing promotional copy and you don't have to pay an expert copywriter to make your product or service stand out. You don't need to have a background in marketing and you don't need an English degree. If you are prepared to put in some time and effort you can teach yourself how to write great copy. When you understand how copywriting works you'll see that with some moderate effort on your part you can pull it off and save yourself a lot of money.

A sales page on your website is any page that promotes your product or service. Think about all the reasons why someone wouldn't want to buy your product or service and make your copy answer those concerns as they read through the page. There are also reasons why someone has come to your site and you must tell them upfront exactly what problem your product or service solves for them. To get them to read your copy you need to start right at the top with a really attention grabbing headline. The headline is the most often read part of your sales page and will determine whether someone reads any further.

With a little time and effort spent practicing simple and practical copywriting strategies you could easily become the expert copywriter for your business, because only you are the expert on your business. After all it's your idea, you have lived and breathed it and now it's time to put all your passion into words by writing copy that *sells*.

Here are some tips about what your headline should do.

6 TOP TIPS FOR HEADLINES
1. Make your headline speak to your ideal customer.

Your headline needs to grab the attention of the customer you want to attract and single them out. For example if you want holiday home owners, your headline could begin with *"Florida Holiday Home Owners! Discover How to get more Rentals Quickly and Easily!"*

The more narrow the criteria the lower quantity of responses but you should get more quality responses - your ideal prospects.

2. Get straight to the point - offer the benefits or a promise to the reader.

Answer the question everyone has on their mind, *"What's in it for me?"* and your ideal customer will take notice.

3. Arouse curiosity so the reader is inclined to keep reading.

However you don't want your headline just to be some trick to get people to read. If you can combine curiosity with benefits for the reader you have a great headline. Don't try to be too clever, creative, obscure or funny – people are just too busy to work out what it's really all about and you could lose their attention.

4. Offer news if possible.

News is always a good attention-getter. Everybody likes to stay current. So announcements like new developments, improvements, new procedures, new launch work well. Think about how you can come up with a news hook and state it loud and clear.

5. Suggest a simple and fast way to get results.

A quick and easy way can be irresistible, but don't mislead and be careful that what you are claiming is believable. Here are some of the general results that people want.

- To be: healthier, slimmer, fitter, a better parent, more educated, happier, superior.
- To save: time, money.
- To have: convenience, better relationships, security, more freedom, a purpose, status.
- To avoid: worry, stress.
- To look good, feel good, influence people, be successful and contribute more.

6. Use influential power words.

Certain words can make your headline influential. Some of the most simple yet powerful words are "you", "how", "new" and "How to". If you are stuck for a headline the classic "How to..." is still working amazingly well. Here are some other power words to try:

✓ Amazing	✓ Announcing
✓ Advice to	✓ At last
✓ Annoying	✓ Bargain
✓ Discover	✓ Do You
✓ Easy	✓ Fast
✓ Facts	✓ Free
✓ Here	✓ Hate
✓ How much	✓ How would
✓ Introducing	✓ Just
✓ Love	✓ Now
✓ Only	✓ Protect
✓ Quick	✓ Sale
✓ Secrets to	✓ Simple
✓ The Truth about	✓ Why
✓ Yes	

Experiment with using a few power words in your headline – for example:

*"At last! New Simple Online
Marketing System Discovered"*

or

*"The truth about advertising – the facts you must
know before you spend another penny on advertising"*

Now it's your turn. Here's an exercise to help you create a headline for your business.

MY HEADLINE

1. Who's attention do you want to grab?
2. What's in it for them?
3. Which power words can you use?
4. Put it all together now to create your headline

From now on be really interested in headlines you see in magazines and newspapers because they are a great source of inspiration for you when you are thinking about creating your own headlines. Take notice of the ones that really grab your attention and ask yourself, *"why?"* Then ask yourself, *"How can I adapt that headline to suit my business/service/product/target market?"* Chances are that by simply replacing some of the words with ones that relate to your business you'll have created a great headline instantly!

Don't stick with the first headline you create just keep writing them out until you dry up then choose which one grabs you the most. There's no rule about how long your headline should be just make it as long as it needs to be to make it sell for you.

HOW TO CREATE SUPER COPY

So now you've got your powerful, attention grabbing headline and your reader is intrigued to learn more you don't want to disappoint them with the rest of your page! Here's a great way to think about your sales copy - the purpose of your first sentence is to make people want to read the second sentence. And the purpose of the second sentence is to make people read the third sentence, etc.

Keep that simple fact in mind whenever you are writing your sales page or a sales letter.

A simple test for writing good copy is to read it out loud. Another simple test is to have someone else read it to you. Preferably someone who knows nothing about what your are selling and if you have an 11 year old at home then this is an ideal job for them. That doesn't mean that you think your potential customers have the mind of an 11 year old! It simply means that if your sales copy can be read and understood by an 11 year old then it will be quick and easy to read by a website visitor who might click away if you don't grab their attention.

Continue to use power words throughout the rest of your copy and apply these strategies:

- Write like you talk and almost as if you were talking to a friend.
- Show enthusiasm – because you aren't meeting your reader face to face you need to put passion into your copy.
- It's all about them – your reader needs to feel that you are writing to them personally so use 'you' and 'your' throughout.
- Keep sentences and paragraphs short and simple which is easier to read and much more inviting than long blocks of words.
- Use subheadings like mini headlines to break up long blocks of words and keep the reader's attention. Also subheads can still get your sales message across if a reader just scans the page.
- Use graphics to draw attention to important points like: Bullets, numbering 1,2,3, <u>underlining,</u> *italics*, **bold**, ALL CAPITALS and highlighting.
- Tell your story about why you are selling your product or service.

- Use testimonials from other customers.
- Tell your reader what you want them to do – what action do you want them to take after reading your sales page? Sign up now? Click here now? Buy now? Join now?

THE 3 STEP PROBLEM-AGITATION-SOLUTION FORMULA

The "problem-agitation-solution" formula is a simple and effective way to get your prospective customers motivated to do something about their problem by triggering an emotional state. First you should understand that people generally want to avoid pain as much as possible and that's what drives them to take action.

Here is the formula:

Step 1 - Define your customer's pain or problem

For example a personal trainer's prospective customer's pain triggers could be: Looking older than they are because of excess weight. Being too tired to play with the kids. Or maybe they've tried all kinds of diets and still can't lose weight.

Step 2 - Agitate the problem

Doing this really stirs up their emotions. They realise how much they are suffering and nothing they have done or are doing is solving their problem. Here's how a personal trainer might do it:

"You can starve yourself on the latest faddy diet but you still won't get rid of that bulge that's robbing you of your energy and confidence!"

Step 3 - Offer the solution

You are exactly what they have been looking for, hoping for, wishing for and dreaming of!

Now it's your turn. Thinking about your product or service and the problem that it solves create your own sales copy. Here's an exercise to help you.

MY SALES COPY

1. What is your target customer's pain and/or problem? What words can you use to make them think 'that's me'?
2. Agitate the problem. Come up with a sentence or two using powerful words that will stir emotions.
3. How does your product or service solve the problem? What are the benefits to be gained?

If this is your first exposure to how writing copy really works you might be wondering if it's really necessary to go into all this detail. Well, don't just take my word for it. Start noticing sales copy and see for yourself that this formula is so effective and is widely used by the best copywriters. The next time you get junk mail don't throw it straight in the bin. Read it for research purposes and notice how the letter uses copy.

Another way to see some quick selling techniques is on shopping channels. The presenter has to make a compelling sales presentation along the lines of this formula in very little time and it's worth taking a look with your mumpreneur head on.

Take particular notice on sales pages, letters or presentations about what happens at the end. What action are you being asked to take?

Make it clear what prospects need to do get the benefits and results you have shown them. It is your responsibility to make sure people who have read through your sales copy will take the next step. It's only human nature to procrastinate so don't hide the solution that you promised in your copy.

SUPERTIP

Try out your sales message on your kids. Or your mum! If they can understand the benefits of your business you've cracked it.

MAKE AN OFFER THEY CAN'T REFUSE!

There are two ways for you to use sales copy on your website. The first sales copy a visitor is likely to see will be the copy on your home page which can use all the strategies you have learned so far with the objective of converting a lead to a prospect on your list.

The other sales copy you will need is to sell products or services directly from your site. Your sales copy needs to answer almost all the questions a prospect might have so that they are not confused and compelled to take action. Remember the reason you have a website is to automate much of your business. If your website does a good job of selling what you offer you'll eliminate the need for prospects to call you to find out more which is not good use of your time and not theirs either. Also if a client needs to call to take it further are they going to be able to reach you? Realistically how available can you be to answer every call? Good sales copy with perhaps an FAQ – frequently asked questions will help your website visitor decide if what you are offering is right for them.

The objective of sales copy for a direct order is to direct the reader straight to a sale. You want to arouse so much interest that before the reader has even got to the end they are wondering how much it costs or how they buy it!

If you have answered all of your reader's questions, concerns and objections in your sales copy then making your offer is the last simple step. The key is to build up so much value that by the time the reader gets to the cost they feel like they are getting a good deal.

There are two steps you can take at the end of your sales copy to improve sales:

1. Summarise exactly what they get including the benefits.
2. Give them a bonus.

It's no secret! Offering something for nothing as a condition of a sale is a widely used strategy. From your supermarket offering buy-one-get-one-free, to your car dealer offering a sunroof in with the deal. Have you really thought about how you could offer bonuses to your customers? This needs to be part of your ongoing sales strategy. The quickest and easiest bonuses for you to offer are digital products or e-books which can be downloaded instantly after the sale. Here are some other ideas for bonuses:

- Special Report
- Quick Start Guide
- Checklist
- Audio Recording
- Questionnaire
- Article

**SUPERTIP**

It's not about YOU it's about THEM! Arouse curiosity about your product or service by asking questions.

THE P.S.

Don't forget your P.S. in any letter. The P.S. is the second most read part of the letter, after the headline. So it makes sense to spend some time and come up with a compelling P.S. Think of the P.S. as your second headline. You can use it to reinforce a key selling point or tell people not to miss out by a certain deadline.

P.S. Don't send a letter without a P.S.!

OFFER A GUARANTEE

Despite all the thought and effort you have put in to get leads from your target market and turn them into prospects there may still be some resistance to buying.

There are many different personal reasons why a prospect who is interested in your service or product may be hesitant about going through with a sale. Maybe they're still not sure if it's what they really need. Maybe they have to justify buying it to someone else like a partner or a bookkeeper. Maybe they are afraid of being conned out of money. If only they knew for sure that if they weren't happy they would get their money back – a guarantee.

By offering a guarantee with all sales you are putting your prospect at ease and giving them no more reasons *not* to buy. It will give you more confidence when selling and will give the prospect more confidence in buying. You can market your product or service on the strength of a guarantee. Take away the risk to the customer by offering a powerful guarantee. Examples are a money back guarantee, a penalty guarantee where you guarantee a customer you'll pay them a certain amount if their time has been wasted by you and a free replacement guarantee.

Be daring with your guarantee and don't be concerned that all your customers will want their money back! Okay maybe you'll have a small percentage of dissatisfied customers. You just have to refund them with no hard feelings. It will happen eventually and you may have to give a few refunds, so you might as well turn your guarantee into a positive sales message. Honouring your guarantees will help you to build your integrity with your market. The point is that having a strong guarantee gives you great confidence when selling your product or service and your customers have more confidence in their decision to buy from you with no risk.

A SALES LETTER TEMPLATE

Headline

Introduction outlining Problem

Agitate Problem

Solution including benefits and overcome any objections

Testimonials from satisfied customers

Guarantee

Most Wanted Response

P.S.

UPSELL

So now your prospect is convinced that your product or service is exactly what they need and because their purchase is guaranteed they reach for their credit card. At this point they are ready, willing and able to buy and more open to a suggestion to buy more.

Upselling is a common sales strategy and it's an easy way to increase the value of a sales transaction simply by asking for more. Start noticing how often your are encouraged to buy more, like the next time you go to your local coffee shop and get asked, *"Would you like some cookies or pastries to go with your latte?"* Even if you had no intention of having some cookies now that you are at the till and ready to pay for your coffee it's very tempting to say *'yes'*, isn't it?

The point at which a customer has already made a commitment to buy from you is when they are most open to buy more. Be creative and think about how you could upsell a supersize version of your products or service.

Here are some ideas to get you started:

- Buy another for ½ price
- Recommend similar products
- Combine with other products
- Offer with a personal consultation
- Offer a membership trial
- Offer tickets/course/workshop at a discount

Now it's your turn. Here's an exercise to help you create some upsell versions of your product or service.

MY UPSELL

Come up with three different ways that you could upsell more of your products or services...

1. _____

2. _____

3. _____

REJECTION – GET OVER IT!

Okay so having your website do the selling for you is great because you don't have to deal with rejection right? Wrong! The brutal truth is that you'll get rejected a lot more by website visitors than you will selling face to face. It's so easy for a visitor to just click away from your site and you'll never know they were there – until you see your stats!

Take your website conversion seriously and keep your eye on how you can constantly improve the number of sign ups. Visitors who are not signing up are rejecting you for one reason or another. To get some real world perspective on selling your product or service you have to get out there and sell directly. Ironically your success online will be affected by your activities offline!

Don't hide behind your website too much. Even though you have all your products and services listed on your website and that's where you take orders you're still going to need to sell the website to people. For example you could attend an exhibition where you sell some products directly from your stand and also sell the benefits of visiting your website and ask for contact details to get some leads. The chances are you are going to face a fair amount of rejection from the masses of people attending. Not everyone who stops by your stand is going to buy so expect it to happen and it won't be so much of a shock. It's not personal so why not see the funny side and see how many rejections it takes before you get a sale!

Fear of rejection is hard wired into all of us and it's just not true that you have to wait until you are more confident at selling to start selling. The difference between being brave and being a coward is that a brave person actually does what they are afraid to do. If you are afraid of selling because of rejection just do it and your confidence will grow as a result.

Think about it this way – facing and dealing with rejection will make you the best salesperson for your business! Having to think on your feet, be creative in your approach, have a sense of humour about it all will result in you naturally turning into a confident and self-assured sales person. That's exactly how all the top performing salespeople have succeeded. They just had to get going, be clunky at first and get better.

WARM CALLING

Do you like receiving cold calls? I'm guessing not! Why is that? Probably because not only have you been disturbed while you are cooking dinner but because you instantly feel under pressure from the salesperson. Even if they are softly spoken and apologise for disturbing you, when they go straight into a sales pitch you just feel like hanging up.

A typical cold call starts something like, "Good evening. I'm John from John's Company. We offer X and we do Y..." this shouts SCRIPT and you just know that unless you stop them right there they are going to go through their whole sales script with you with the intention of closing a sale or getting an appointment.

The problem with this whole cold calling approach is not only relying on a script for 'conversation' but that the salesperson has assumed that you are interested in their product or service and they have a list of one liners to use in response to any objections you have.

The next time you get a cold call why not respond to their introduction with "Oh Hi John. How are you?" and see how they struggle to have a natural conversation with you without using their script. Cold calling can sound and feel fake because it doesn't fit with our everyday language and can seem forced causing resistance. I call it 'putting in the tape' because it can sound like a machine talking to you.

During my time as a Sales Trainer some of us had a joke about working for the Sales Prevention Department because the sales process adopted by the company was very scripted, allowed for little flexibility and conversation and was all about getting to the close. If any objections were brought up, which were probably said just to get rid of us, there was yet another sales aid full of 'clever' responses to overcome the objection, get the sales pitch back on track and get to the close.

I never did feel comfortable or genuine with that kind of approach to selling and to be honest the top performers had got such outstanding results usually by putting effort in to build a relationship with many of their customers based on mutual respect and co-operation.

Being my own Sales Department means I can communicate with people about my business by simply being myself and not putting pressure on myself or prospects to get a 'close'.

There are going to be many opportunities in your business for you to make cold calls, in other words, calling people who know nothing about you, your business and what you do. It's likely to be leads or prospects but it could be a journalist or maybe someone you would like to affiliate with. Remember that you want to be perceived as a problem solver, a trusted advisor and a helpful salesperson. To increase your chances of getting what you want do some research before you make the call – do you really have something that person needs? What problems do they have that you could help with? The call should be all about *them* not, "we are this, we do that, we have this to offer".

To avoid having barriers put up at the start of the call try to open by introducing your-self then ask, "I wonder if you can help me?" This approach usually gets you a positive response like, "I'll try" or "Yes, how?"

Now you can ask a question relating to their problems like, "Would you be interested in hearing about a solution to you problems with XYZ?" What you are trying to do is open up the conversation around how your product or service can help them. Forget about a script but keep in mind 3 key points that you want to include in your conversation.

Consider the call as potentially the start of a long term relationship and work out whether taking it further is a good use of your time and their time. If there is an objection don't dismiss it. You don't know the other person's circumstances and they may have a genuine issue with financial or time constraints so show respect by helping them to understand how your product or service will help. If they are showing interest give them space to make the decision to buy or agree by suggesting, "What's the next step" or "What would you like to do now?"

Here are the key points to making a 'warm' call.

HOW TO MAKE A WARM CALL

- Make sure the call is about them – not you.
- Introduce yourself and ask if they can help you.
- Ask a question about problems they need a solution to.
- Include 3 key points about your product or service in the conversation.
- Help them to understand how your product or service will help.
- Ask them what they would like to do next.

Don't be tempted to always send an e-mail instead of making a call. You are probably afraid of rejection again. Despite e-mail being a great advantage to your online business the problem with e-mailing instead of calling is you can't make a natural conversation from an e-mail. What happens if you send an e-mail and get no reply? It's harder for you to pick up the phone after being 'rejected' by e-mail. If you call first, have a conversation then you can always use an e-mail as a back up to send more information.

If you do have to send a cold e-mail use the problem solving approach instead of blatantly pitching who you are, your company name and what you do.

KEY POINTS

- With all sales there is a critical *motivating factor* that makes people buy and to make a sale you need to find out or work out what that is for your customer. Motivating factors are the emotions that someone has connected with buying the product or service.
- By asking the right questions you can give the best advice and being perceived as an advisor or expert

will help you to build some trust with potential customers. Another great way for you to be successful in selling to make people feel like they are being taught about your product or service.

- Because you are not there in person to greet your website visitors, ask questions and assist them you need to sell yourself and the benefits of your product or service with short, clear and precise words that communicate your message *and* answer their questions- *your copy.*

- To get them to read your copy you need to start right at the top with a really attention grabbing headline because this is the most read part of your sale.

- Here's a great way to think about your sales copy - the purpose of your first sentence is to make people want to read the second sentence. And the purpose of the second sentence is to make people read the third sentence, etc.

- The "problem-agitation-solution" formula is a simple and effective way to get your prospective customers motivated to do something about their problem by triggering an emotional state. First you should understand that people generally want to avoid pain as much as possible and that's what drives them to take action.

- You want to arouse so much interest that before the reader has even got to the end they are wondering how much it costs or how they buy it! If you have answered all of your readers questions, concerns and objections already in your sales copy then making your offer is the last simple step.

- Think of the P.S. as your second headline. You can use it to reinforce a key selling point or tell people not to miss out by a certain deadline.
- By offering a guarantee with all sales you are putting your prospect at ease and giving them no more reasons *not* to buy. It will give you more confidence when selling and will give the prospect more confidence in buying.
- The point at which a customer has already made a commitment to buy from you is when they are most open to buy more. Be creative and think about how you could upsell a supersize version of your products or service.
- If you are afraid of selling because of rejection just do it and your confidence will grow as a result. Think about it this way – facing and dealing with rejection will make you the best salesperson for your business!
- There are going to be many opportunities in your business for you to make cold calls. It's likely to be leads or prospects but it could be a journalist or maybe someone you would like to affiliate with. Remember that you want to be perceived as a problem solver, a trusted advisor and a helpful salesperson.
- Forget about a script but keep in mind 3 key points that you want to include in your conversation. Consider the call as potentially the start of a long term relationship and work out whether taking it further is a good use of your time and their time.

Marketing Campaigns

"The Fortune is in the Follow Up."

Now that you understand how critical the sales and marketing part of your business are and have some simple strategies to get you started you can step it up by running a marketing campaign. A series of co-ordinated marketing strategies could result in a surge of new customers and help your business to grow faster. You can maintain all the marketing activities so far and add on a campaign to take advantage of a new launch, a sale, seasonal promotions or some hot news.

Here are some ideas for different marketing campaigns:

REFERRALS CAMPAIGN

Call some of your best customers and ask them what else they need from you. This will give you ideas on expanding your business. Then simply ask them for two referrals.

Do a referral campaign for all your existing customers and prospects by offering something of value to them for free in return for two referrals.

Of course it's going to be much easier for you to get these referrals if you have earned them through delivering an outstanding service. If you give an outstanding service people will naturally tell others about you. These days, as service is generally getting worse, you have a great opportunity to stand out because of the service you deliver. That one factor in your business could lead to your customers referring you to others.

PUBLIC SPEAKING CAMPAIGN

It's the No.1 fear in the US and UK! Even more of a reason for you to overcome the fear and master this very important skill. Go back to Success Mindset to remind yourself about how to master fear.

Purposefully put yourself in the uncomfortable situation of talking to a group of people of whom some could be future customers. The majority of people wait until they feel confident enough to deliver a presentation. The fact is that it's only by delivering a presentation that you will start to gain confidence. You can practice in the mirror and procrastinate as much as you like but the skill will only be developed by doing it for real.

Research 10 groups of potential customers and find out when they are having their meetings. Even if it's a small group in your local community, just do it. Get started. Offer to be a guest speaker and give useful information before promoting your service or product at the end. Nothing leaves more of an impact on people than an in-person presentation and people will remember you when they have your presentation in their mind.

At each event that you speak at take advantage of having leads in the audience by asking for e-mail addresses in return for your freebie. You can then either sign them up to your list or e-mail them with a link to your site reminding them to pick up their free gift.

PR CAMPAIGN

In our 'celeb' culture today it's more important than ever to seek out any opportunity for some publicity - *PR*. Exploit PR and make it a consistent part of your marketing strategy.

Think about seeing an article or feature about a business in a magazine or newspaper compared to seeing an advertisement. For example if you were interested in going on a cookery course and a magazine you were reading had a feature article about a new course with some photos and in the classifieds section there was another course provider advertising, which would have the most impact on you? Generally people are more impressed by reading an article or interview perhaps with additional unbiased comments and images than seeing an advertisement for the same business. Having an article published or being featured in a newspaper or magazine can also you more credibility than paying for an advert in a publication.

Don't be mistaken by thinking that getting PR is all about ego. The exposure that you and your business gets from PR means you can influence more people in your target market with just one good article or feature than any advert ever could. PR is just another way of generating leads and people will be curious and compelled to check out your website or product. Seeing your picture in a magazine, hearing you on the radio and watching you on TV gives people the feeling that you are for real, like they already know you and they will be more likely to trust.

The media needs stories - so give them one! Get a press release done and get it out there. You can always practice working with the media by getting your business written about in your local paper or community magazine. If the thought of being interviewed fills you with terror then just like the public speaking it's only by doing interviews that you'll grow in confidence.

It's worth investing some time to explore how you could develop a PR campaign for your business and I could write another book just on that subject. There are plenty of PR resources which can help you to do it all yourself such as *www.doyourownpr.com.*

Plan your campaigns at least 3 months in advance. When the kids are back to school in September you need to be planning your Christmas and New Year campaigns.

DIRECT MAIL CAMPAIGN

What's the first thing you think of when you hear 'Direct Mail'?

I bet you're thinking 'junk mail'. Direct mail is only junk mail if people are not interested in what has been sent to them. If you have carefully selected who you are targeting with direct mail and provide them with valuable information, you are not sending junk mail. Despite technology making it easier for us to automate our business and communicate with our customers by e-mail don't ignore the good old-fashioned snail mail way of contacting your customers - *direct mail.* One of the problems with e-mail is that it's so easy for your prospect or customer to click – delete – click – delete. How do you know that they have read your message? How long might it sit in their inbox? They might read it and be interested then start surfing the net and get distracted.

E-mail addresses change quicker than direct mail addresses and some of your e-mail addresses will end up as undeliverable when people start using a new e- mail address.

For the best results from marketing you need to be combining your online marketing with offline marketing. Creating a direct mail campaign from scratch is simple when you know how and can bring you a rush of new business and that's why so many businesses still use direct mail.

Notice all the direct mail that comes to you and instead of throwing it in the bin take a look to see what sales techniques are used in the sales letter. Sales letters are ideal for generating leads, attracting new customers and reactivating old or lost customers. Once you have a proven direct mail letter you can continue mailing it to more and more people with the same successful results. Just imagine if you could hire someone who will relentlessly go out to deliver your message perfectly every time, never call in sick and never moan — all for the time it takes you to write a letter while having a cuppa! That's how a sales letter can work for you.

You can start off small, mailing as few as 500 or 1000 letters at first, and then expand as the money starts coming in. Pound for pound direct mail provides the best return on investment.

Think about what campaigns you could run in your business. Taking advantage of seasonal events is always a good one. Be creative like offering your customers a discount because it's your birthday. The experts in direct mail make a 12-month plan of different campaigns to run throughout the year. There is a process and certain techniques to use when running a direct mail campaign that I'll share with you.

HOW TO DO A DIRECT MAIL CAMPAIGN

For the best results you'll need 3 parts of your direct mail campaign in place:

1. Your List
2. Your Style
3. Your Offer

The Mother of All Lists

Mail with a label on it that says, "To the homeowner" or, "resident" is junk mail. If people have never indicated they are interested in your products or services, nor have you qualified them as good targets for your offerings then don't waste your time sending mail to them. When you have built up a list of prospects and customers you have the perfect opportunity to run a direct mail campaign because you have the ideal list. It's the list that too often gets neglected with direct mail and you must have all of your customer's names and addresses in a database (try to get addresses from prospects too). This list will be the best and most responsive list you can use for any offers because these people have already bought from you, trust you and like doing business with you.

If you're in a type of business that typically doesn't keep customer names and addresses it's really important that *you* do otherwise you're missing an incredible opportunity to create more business. Typically businesses like restaurants and retail shops never collect customer's names and addresses.

Have you ever had a letter from one of your favourite restaurants inviting you back? It's much more cost effective to sell more to people who have already bought from you than to 'buy' new customers.

Personal Style

Your objective when you are creating your direct mail campaign is to grab your prospect's or customer's attention and get them to actually open the letter. People are not eagerly awaiting your sales letter and when they do receive it they will have a number of things on their mind as they pick up the mail like:

"More bills! Oh have I paid the credit card bill yet?"

"Look at the time! I'm going to be late if I don't get a move on."

"I need to get to the supermarket sometime today. What am I going to make for tea?"

"Junk mail...junk...junk...oh...what's this? It looks like a personal letter. I wonder who it's from?"

Make your letter look personal by using a real stamp and a handwritten address – a great job for older children to earn their pocket money or to delegate to willing family members or friends! The aim is to try and avoid your letter being discarded immediately as junk and sent to the recycling bin. Or if you'd prefer use your company's branded envelopes and labels to get attention. This is the time to get really creative with the design to give your copy the best chance of getting read. You could outsource the task of designing your materials to a freelance designer for example through *www.elance.com*. A simple postcard can be really effective, especially if there is an image that just can't be thrown away on the front!

SUPERTIP

A funny postcard or cartoon in a sales letter can help your message to get read *and* might even end up on your customer's fridge or wall!

Sequential Mailing

The key to success with a direct mail campaign is consistently following-up. Plan to send a sequence of letters to get the best results because a response rate of under 10% is common with direct mail. For example you could get a 5% response from your first letter but another 6% from a second letter and a further 7% from a third letter. If you don't follow up after sending one letter you'll be losing out on additional sales. Most people that try a direct mail campaign only use a one letter mailing. It is much more difficult to make a one letter campaign work well, especially to a list that don't know anything about you.

It's not unusual to get an even greater response on your second letter. Send out your second letter about 2-3 weeks after the first sales letter has gone out. There could be many people who wanted to respond but just never quite got around to it. Your letter might have ended up in a pile of mail, bills, etc. So when your second letter comes reminding them of the deadline to respond they take action this time around.

Offer With A Deadline

Putting an irresistible offer in your letter is another way to improve the results of your direct mail campaign. It needs to be such a good offer that people would be crazy not to take you up on it. Think of the most fantastic offer you can and if you get stuck just remember, everyone likes to get something for free.

This is another way that you could use your freebie from your website. Instead of a download you could professionally print and package an information product to offer as a lead generator. These kind of information products will cost you a little to produce but will have a high perceived value and are a great way to position yourself as an expert.

Your prospects are being bombarded with information daily and your offer is probably not at the top of their mind. Your letter has to make them take action and respond right now! Avoid just giving your phone number and leaving it up to the prospect or customer to call you sometime, when they get round to it. You must make it absolutely clear what prospects need to do in order to get the benefits and results you have told them about in your letter.

A very effective method for getting action is a specific deadline. It's best if you have a reason for the deadline, like you have to sell out of a certain amount of stock by a specific date. Another strategy is to set a limit on the amount of people eligible for the offer like the first 50 who respond. Scarcity produces good results too by letting them know that you only have so many to sell and when they're gone – that's it.

WHAT MAKES A DIRECT MAIL CAMPAIGN SUCCESSFUL?

When you analyse the results of your direct mail campaign don't get too hung up on percentages and stop to remind yourself of the objective of the campaign - to make money. Suppose you had sent out 3000 letters and you only got a 1% response rate of 30. You might decide that this was an unsatisfactory result and that your campaign was unsuccessful. Look closer at the numbers and work out what the average annual spend is per customer in your business. In this case we'll say a customer spends on average £150 per year with you.

SUPERTIP

Make your own 'swipe file' of sales letters, leaflets and any other marketing materials to give you inspiration when creating your own campaigns.

Now you have 30 people who responded to your sales letter and are worth on average £150 each as a new customer. So actually your direct mail campaign has gained you £4500 worth of business. Allow £1000 for mailing costs and you still have a net of £3500. Not bad for just sending a couple of letters!

Understand that a customer is worth more to you than just a one off sale because the more higher cost products and services you have to offer the more you can move them through your 'marketing funnel' and new customers can send you many more by referring you to others. Your customer list is your most lucrative business asset.

KEY POINTS

- You can maintain all the marketing activities so far and add on a campaign to take advantage of a new launch, a sale, seasonal promotions or some hot news.
- Do a referral campaign for all your existing customers and prospects by offering something of value to them for free in return for 2 referrals.
- Nothing leaves more of an impact on people than an in-person presentation. Offer to be a guest speaker and give useful information before promoting your service or product at the end.
- The exposure that you and your business get from PR means you can influence more people in your target market with just one good article or feature than any advert ever could.
- Creating a direct mail campaign from scratch is simple when you know how and can bring you a rush of new business. That's why so many businesses still use direct mail.
- Your customer list is your most lucrative business asset.

Mumentum

"Most people are fast to stop you BEFORE you get started but hesitant to get in the way if you are moving."

TIM FERRIS - THE 4 HOUR WORK WEEK

If you conceived your idea months ago it might seem to be taking a lifetime to get your business out there into the big wide world. All the effort you have been putting in, the months of research and still you feel like you have nothing to show for it. Take heart because what you have been doing is building momentum and just like riding a bike it requires energy and forward motion to get things moving.

At the start you might have no contacts, no customers and no track record and it can be de-motivating when it seems like nothing is happening. You keep looking around for opportunities, ways to bring in new business and a foot in the door somewhere. It's relentless, time consuming and at the time not even rewarding because nobody knows you, nobody believes in you and still you feel like nothing is happening.

Stick with it because with each passing day, every contact you make, each phone call, each e-mail and each meeting is moving you closer to your goal and you are silently building momentum.

Then one day you finally get a breakthrough – you get your first online sale, you sign a contract or get your first client and you never forget the first! This gives you a boost in confidence and gives you a surge of energy to keep going with more conviction. Once you get going it doesn't take long for the momentum to build up so that opportunities start coming to you in twos and threes.

Be open to new ideas, new opportunities, new information and new people that come your way from your efforts. Think of this momentum that you have created as a wave of opportunity. It's that wonderful feeling you get when things are going well, moving in the right direction and happening fast. It's like a snowball effect - *you're on a roll*! Take what has come to you and ride it, run with it and milk it for all it's worth!

Don't hesitate when this happens to you because the wave will only last so long if you don't keep it going. Momentum is produced when you focus with intensity on a goal and consistently pursue that goal. Like riding that bike again you have to start peddling to get the wheels moving but if you stop peddling eventually you will slow down and stop. You need to have momentum to help you stay on track because slowing down can cause you to doubt yourself or even worse, to become complacent.

 **SUPERTIP**

Expose yourself! Create or take advantage of opportunities to expose your name and your business to gain recognition and build momentum.

You are responsible for continuing to build the momentum in your business by staying strong and steady all the time. Keep making progress, keep challenging yourself, so long as you don't stop. Even just a little every day, a little at a time is better than stopping. There will be setbacks that appear in many different forms like financial setbacks, conflicts, and unforeseen circumstances - so expect them. These are sent to test you and to see just how resilient you are.

All successful people have had to cope with and persevere through setbacks – it's all part of the route to success and hardly anybody gets there in a straight line - so don't give up. Being a mum has given you plenty of experience of crisis management so far and you'll end up stronger and wiser in your business after turning things around.

Remain open to opportunities because they will always come your way if you are ready for them. *Attract* opportunity and it will find you through other people.

CAN I TELL YOU A SECRET?

Have you heard of *The Secret*? It's the title of a movie and a book and the secret is the law of attraction. *The Secret* says it's the most powerful law of all the Universal laws and that we *attract* everything in our lives through the magnetic power of our thoughts. According to *The Secret* we don't get what we *do* want because our *dominant* thoughts are about what we *don't* want:

"I don't want to fail"

"I don't want to be sad"

"I can't cope with all this work"

This doesn't mean that you have to keep monitoring your thoughts all day – that's a quick way to wear yourself out. Your *feelings* will tell you what you are thinking because our feelings are the effect of our thoughts.

The creative process used in *The Secret* states that you create whatever you want in your life using these 3 steps:

- Step 1: Ask the Universe for what you want
- Step 2: Believe that it's already yours
- Step 3: Receive and feel the way you will feel when it happens

So there you go, just ask the Universe for a million quid and forget about all this business stuff! If only it were that easy! I'm not suggesting that the Law of Attraction isn't true and I do actually believe there is something in it. I've noticed many connections in my life, I've attracted situations and experiences almost exactly as I had imagined them.

The thing is you can sit and think about what you want and ask for it all day long but if you don't actually *do* something to put yourself in a position to receive it how will you realistically get what you want? If you really did want that million quid I doubt that someone will come knocking on your door with a cheque or that you will win the lottery! However, starting a business just might be the way that the million quid will eventually find its way to you. Business success always comes back down to the same thing – *taking action*.

SUPERTIP

Be flexible. As your business grows you might decide to re-brand yourself and your business. Don't think you got it wrong at the start. It's all part of making progress.

KEY POINTS

- Each passing day, every contact you make, each phone call, each e-mail and each meeting is moving you closer to your goal and you are silently building momentum.

- Once you get going it doesn't take long for the momentum to build up so that opportunities start coming to you in twos and threes.

- Momentum is produced when you focus with intensity on a goal and consistently pursue that goal.

- Keep making progress, keep challenging yourself, so long as you don't stop. Even just a little every day, a little at a time is better than stopping.

- We *attract* everything in our lives through the magnetic power of our thoughts.

- You can sit and think about what you want and ask for it all day long but if you don't actually *do* something to put yourself in a position to receive it how will you realistically get what you want?

- Business success always comes back down to the same thing – *taking action*.

You're Fired!

"Plan for your future because that's where you are going to spend the rest of your life."

MARK TWAIN

Your business needs you to give it your care and attention to help it grow big and strong and able to stand on it's own feet. As soon as it's up and running it doesn't need you to carry it so much and that's your time to pull back and think about how you can help your business to mature and become independent with help and guidance from you. Before you even start you need to understand that to avoid becoming more stressed out and burned out more than ever you need to get your business to a point where it is not dependant on you. As soon as you possible start weaning your business from needing you to be there every day, to running smoothly without you because of the systems you have put in place.

SUPERTIP

When the going gets tough be grateful for what you have and with all the tragedy in the world be grateful that you have your children. Where would you be without them?

Imagine never being able to go on holiday because you're terrified of the business collapsing without you or worse going on holiday but spending it as a walking nervous breakdown on the phone and checking e-mail trying in vain to remain in control. What if there were a tragedy? Life has a habit of throwing some nasty surprises and you'll be in a much stronger position to cope with any crap that comes your way if your business can run without you temporarily.

A system is something that consistently delivers the same result. Put systems into your business which others can be trained in so they can deliver the same result as you by using your system. Or get some software to deliver for you in your absence. You need people to be able to do business with your company while you are having the time of your life queuing at Disneyworld!

An important system is one that means you personally do not have to attract customers. If all new business can only be obtained by you in person then you are setting a trap for yourself. This is the reason why you need to focus on outsourcing tasks and automation so that your marketing, your website, your ordering system and your team can all keep your business in business.

Even though you may be raring to go for it what excites you now may not be so exciting to you in five years time – or less. Avoid jumping from the frying pan of full time work and into the fire of a business that has you even more trapped. The ultimate purpose for starting your own business while being a mum *must* be for freedom – that is what making profits gives you. That's the reward you *deserve* for taking the risk to go into business while raising your young family – for putting all that focussed time in – for the resilience – the determination.

Make no apologies for getting yourself into a position of freedom where you have grown your business into a profitable organisation that has efficient systems and people in place that are not dependant upon you.

Notice that it's the systems and people that are not dependant on you – the success of your business *is* dependant on you. You are of critical significance to your business and to your customers. It's your responsibility to ensure your business delivers what it promises and is profitable – even in your absence.

Success will have a different meaning for all of us and only you will know what success looks like and feels like to you. Imagine that you have 'made it' – what would you choose to do? If you've been conditioned to think that to be successful and wealthy means you are tight and ruthless with money think again. The wealth that business success could bring you means you'll have the freedom to be as generous as you like. Through being a successful mumpreneur you could even find yourself contributing the same amount to your chosen charity as you used to earn in annual salary.

Having freedom doesn't mean you have to adopt some kind of hedonistic lifestyle where all you do is chill out on the beach and drink cocktails either. You'd soon get bored of that – honest!

SUPERTIP

If you're not growing you're rotting! If you are feeling stale, bored, de-motivated, frustrated, resentful or depressed you are not growing.

Freedom to you could mean having the time to grow your own vegetables, start a community group, learn a language, help elderly parents, take up a new interest etc. You'll also have the freedom to apply what you have learned from the experience of running your own business to guide your children and possibly grandchildren in their life decisions.

The normal rules of the 9-5-thank-God-it's-Friday routine don't apply anymore so you can choose to work wherever and whenever you please – as long as the work gets done. Give yourself a break and *fire yourself*!

7 MUST HAVE SYSTEMS

1. New prospect system – what to say and offer to a prospect
2. New customer system- templates, spreadsheets, checklist
3. Monthly accounts checklist
4. Orders checklist
5. Marketing System – implementation procedure
6. Delegation system – who does what
7. Customer service – refund policy, complaints procedure

Now it's your turn. Here's an exercise to help you decide what systems you need in your business.

MY MUST HAVE SYSTEMS

Thinking of your business, decide on the top three systems that MUST put in place NOW...

1. _____

2. _____

3. _____

EMBRACING THE MOBILE MUMPRENEUR LIFESTYLE

One of the most compelling reasons to automate your business online is so that you are able to go walkabout! You're a mum with young children who need you to be there for them and the time is flying by. We demand flexible working from employers but I wonder if flexible jobs for mums really do exist.

Flexible jobs still have to fit with the hours and conditions set by the employer. Yes there are some jobs out there with 'hours to suit' that are mostly commission only sales jobs. Many franchises appeal to mums for the same reason but compared to both of those options I think surely if you are prepared to spend time, and money in the case of buying into a franchise, selling someone else's product or service you would be more successful if that money and effort were put into your own business? For less than what it costs to buy many franchises you could create a business of your own that you really *believe* in and have absolute control over. Like being able to take time out to be with your family.

School holidays are usually a logistical nightmare for many working families, trying to squeeze a little extra time off work or having to plan a week of childcare like a military exercise. Not for you. If your business is online you can access it from anywhere. If your team are outsourced they can access your business from anywhere. Just imagine what a difference being able to work like that could make! You would be able to take lots of mini breaks especially during the school holidays rather than making do with a two-week holiday in the middle of August, then needing a holiday to recover!

Creating your business to fit around your family life is a *lifestyle* choice. It's got nothing to do with being materialistic and bragging about your ten holidays a year. This is about experiencing life, having adventures with your kids, giving them some amazing opportunities to do interesting things. It's about making special memories and it's possible because you run your own business and you have put systems in place so that it can run without you if necessary. Learn to take it easy during these times of work, rest and play. Relax and feel confident that the systems you have in place are keeping your business running smoothly.

You are liberating yourself from the usual concerns about taking time off from a business and other people might try to tell you that it can't be done. Prove them wrong! Block time off in your diary at the beginning of the year and try testing a long weekend to see if it works. Your adventures don't have to be grand and I'm not suggesting that you drag your kids around the world's most luxurious hotels just because you can. Adventures could be a simple camping trip or house swapping with another family.

SUPERTIP

Be an inspiration to your kids. It's the
best gift you could ever give them.

The point is that you have the *freedom* to go on as many as you choose. Take a laptop or use Internet cafes to check in on your business if necessary. Time spent away from your business will help you think about what you want to focus on when you get back and will encourage new and creative ideas to flow.

This is doing the opposite to postponing all your adventures in life until you are retired, the kids have left home and you finally have the time to do what you really wanted to do in your life only now you wished you'd done it years sooner! Business success is your ticket to ride. To have unforgettable experiences with your family.

Because you're not used to thinking like this and living like this it's going to take some practice until it becomes your new lifestyle.

Your business is not the be-all and end-all of your existence. Think of it as a stepping stone. What excites you today might bore the teeth off you in just a couple of years from now. You might decide to take your business in a whole new direction or sell it and start another project or start your own foundation. What's important is that you will have developed the right skills and attitude to be successful in business. Transferable skills that will see you through the rest of your life and will make you the wise old woman at the top of the mountain whom others come to for advice!

 **SUPERTIP**

Be a firm and loving friend to yourself and don't settle for less. Stay focussed on what it is you really want for yourself, your family, and your life.

STEPPING STONES TO SUCCESS

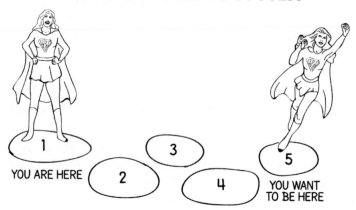

YOU ARE HERE

YOU WANT TO BE HERE

Imagine these 5 stepping stones represent your *pathway* from where you are now to where you want to be. With all change that requires *effort* it's tempting to want to jump straight to where you want to be and *avoid* the discomfort, struggle and challenges along the way. However you *need* the *lessons learned* from stones 1, 2, 3 and 4 to help you maintain your position at stone 5. So what *resources* do you need from stones 2, 3 and 4 to help you get to and *enjoy* being at stone 5?

Here's an exercise to help you.

MY STEPPING STONES TO SUCCESS

Answer the following questions:

1. Where am I at the moment? (Stone 1)
2. Where do I want to be? (Stone 5)
3. What resources do I need to move to stone 2? And to stone 3? Stone 4? Stone 5?
4. How will I know I've 'made it'?

KEY POINTS

- A system is something that consistently delivers the same result. Put systems into your business, which others can be trained in so they can deliver the same result as you. Or get some software to deliver for you in your absence.
- The normal rules of the 9-5-thank-God-it's-friday routine don't apply anymore so you can choose to work wherever and whenever you please – as long as the work gets done.
- Creating your business to fit around your family life is a lifestyle choice.
- Time spent away from your business will help you think about what you want to focus on when you get back and will encourage new and creative ideas to flow.
- The fact is that time is flying by and if you allow yourself to be led by life instead of leading it in the direction you want it to go who knows where you'll end up.

Make it Happen... Now!

"You can have, do, or be anything you want."

DR. JOE VITALE

I learned the hard way from my first experience in business that too much time spent planning, researching and gathering information can result in a slow and frustrating start. Yes information is necessary before you get going but you can actually get to a point of *too much information* and not enough doing. You become stuck with having to spend your precious time ploughing through all that information and sometimes even going over the same ground without actually getting anything done to move your business forward. It's like the 'eternal student syndrome' - taking course after course but never actually getting a job! The planning stage is necessary but can be very time consuming so look for any shortcuts you can.

When I re-launched myself in business I had a different attitude and a new focus about what I wanted to happen in my business and what I needed to do to make it happen. This time round it was all about doing it as *fast* as possible, looking for shortcuts and implementing ideas with speed. The difference was dramatic. It's no surprise that I got much better results from acting on ideas fast compared to dragging it out or worse not focussing on getting it done.

That's why I wrote this book and started Supermummy. To help get you up to speed and to give you shortcuts to simple and effective strategies and 'done-for-you' solutions that you can apply in your business.

It's a myth that it takes three years, five years, ten years – depending who you talk to – for a business to make a profit. Who says that it has to take years before you see profits? It's true that many businesses don't make profits as soon as they start trading and the way that some businesses are set up makes it impossible to make initial profits. It's also true that other businesses are set up with very low costs and make profits quickly. To give yourself the best chance of fast growth and the lifestyle business you want you need to get profits in place right from the start.

Challenge the belief about profits because if you believe that it's going to take three years to make profits then you will behave accordingly. You will unconsciously not act on opportunities that could be lucrative, you might shy away from promoting your business or you could limit what you think you are capable of doing within that time frame because you have convinced yourself that it's just not possible for your business to grow fast.

Give yourself *permission* to succeed quicker than what might have been 'acceptable' to you or others before and believe that it will happen. In our society we still have a hang up about 'get rich quick' thanks to some unscrupulous and greedy business owners. We have been conditioned to think that if your business has made money quickly that you must be doing something wrong, something dishonest or even something illegal! The truth is that it is possible to make money in business quickly – and legally - if it is set up to do so, if you take action and have the right attitude.

Just imagine if you knew for certain that everything you plan to do in the next year *will* happen. How different would you feel about going ahead with your business now with certainty of success? It's the uncertainty and fear that's holding you back and getting in your way. What are you waiting for? Someone to tell you that everything will be ok? Confirmation that you are doing the right thing? Tell yourself! Convince yourself and don't wait any longer.

Be eager to learn from those that have been there already because you don't know it all so make it your business to find out. Read books, go on courses, seminars etc - anything to keep expanding yourself.

Leap rather than crawl to the top because the longer it takes the harder it gets to keep at it, stay motivated and focussed. You want to see some fast results as soon as you launch. If you knew for certain that everything you want to happen will happen what would you want to happen? What goals would you set? What accomplishments? What income? What recognition?

You must have the belief that you *can* and *will* achieve success then take action because action is the link between your dreams and reality. Just think about the amazing progress your baby made in its first year. You nurtured that tiny newborn who just kept growing and growing and with each passing month there was a new delightful development. The first smile, rolling over, the first chuckle, sitting up, crawling, the first teeth, feeding themselves, standing up, the beginnings of the first words and even the first steps. With the same care and attention your business can make big strides towards success even in the first twelve months.

3 MUST DO'S TO MAKING IT HAPPEN

1. Speed Implementation

Your biggest barrier to your success will be lack of implementation. To make progress you must take the *right* action at the *right* time. Slow implementation can take weeks or even months to show any results.

The cause of slow implementation could be feeling low in confidence, having too many distractions, putting things off or simply not knowing what to do and ending up doing nothing.

Speed implementation happens when you have gained enough knowledge or information and focus on taking daily action to implement plans and strategies. This is the time to take advantage of your systems and automation to help you accomplish more. You don't have to do it all yourself and delegating tasks to others will help you to meet deadlines. If you just feel so overwhelmed by the amount of work you need to accomplish simply chunk it down into small manageable tasks that can be done in short bursts.

2. Speed Decision Making

If you aren't already decisive you must purposefully create a new habit. Maybe you've got out of the habit and can't even decide what to make for dinner never mind starting a business!

The best way to create this new habit and get better at making decisions is to start making more of them. Practice with daily small decisions and if you find yourself humming and hahhing just quickly make a decision and stick with it. Then when it comes to running your business you'll be ready to make daily decisions quickly.

To make the right decisions you must ask yourself:

"How much will it cost?"

"How long will it take?"

"How will I make my money back?"

"What can I do today to move closer to my goal?"

"How is doing this going to get me what I really want?"

It's not what you do now and again that will shape your business it's what you do consistently and it all starts with a decision.

3. Speedy Recovery from Setbacks

Don't be defeated by setbacks. They *will* happen and *every* business has them so accept them as part of the journey. Move on and see it as a lesson learned.

After dealing with a setback fill your mind with future plans to avoid letting any self-doubt creep in. Put the situation into perspective because you might be blowing things out of proportion. Sometimes what is a really bad day for you could be seen as a really good day for someone less fortunate. It's also possible that some of your worst days will be the most powerful for you because the experience can give you new strength, commitment and determination to succeed.

Be brave and go forward despite your fears because you'll never know what you were truly capable of if you don't give it your best shot. Stretch yourself beyond the comfortable and you'll discover that what is uncomfortable to you today will soon feel comfortable.

Know what you want to happen in the short term and the long term because sometimes what seems impossible in the short term is possible in the long term. Be persistent and patient if not all your plans work out at the first attempt. What's important is that you get off to a flying start, build momentum quickly and get a boost from some fast results.

Don't allow yourself to get stressed out by the amount of tasks that need to be done. If you're working hard building your business make sure you play hard too. It's important that you have fun with your family because it's the spontaneous and affectionate times with your kids that will keep you sane!

To help you reach your goals and to get you into a 'do it' state of mind for getting to work on your business have reminders around you like:

- Charts – use your kid's reward chart if that works for you!
- Targets – you need to see how you are doing
- Pictures – a photo or image to help you visualise your goals
- Quotes or Words – to inspire you
- Planner – 12 months of fast activity!

 **SUPERTIP**

The hardest part of making a change or starting something new is to take the first step. Keep going and don't look back.

MY "MAKE IT HAPPEN IN 12 MONTHS" PLAN

Take some time now to plan your next twelve months. What do you want to happen in your business? What will you do to make that happen? What has to happen for you to be able to make it happen?

Make a plan now – don't delay, don't put it off and don't put this book down until you have done it!

What Do I Want To Happen?	When Do I Want it to Happen?	What Must I do to Make it Happen?

KEY POINTS

- Information is necessary before you get going but you can actually get to a point of *too much information* and not enough doing.

- The planning stage is necessary but can be very time consuming so look for any shortcuts you can.

- Just imagine if you knew for certain that everything you plan to do in the next year *will* happen. How different would you feel about going ahead with your business now with certainty of success?

- You must have the belief that you can and will achieve success then take action because action is the link between your dreams and reality.

- Speed implementation happens when you have gained enough knowledge or information and focus on taking daily action to implement plans and strategies.

- It's not what you do now and again that will shape your business it's what you do consistently and it all starts with a decision.

- Don't be defeated by setbacks. They *will* happen and *every* business has them so accept them as part of the journey.

- Be persistent and patient if not all your plans work out at the first attempt. What's important is that you get off to a flying start, build momentum quickly and get a boost from some fast results.

- Make a plan now – don't delay.

FROM MY HEART

Supermummy was created out of a genuine respect for mums, like you, and a desire to share what I know to help you. As a mum of three I searched for the ideal work/life balance solution that would allow me to pursue my own interests and ambitions yet still be there for my kids. Setting up an online business made me realise that so many mums out there could really use this too and so it was no longer about me – now it was about us.

And now I have a mission to support all you mums out there to be a Supermummy too!

Remind yourself of your greater purpose as a mum and challenge yourself to be the best role model for your children. When the going gets tough you have a choice about how you are going to respond to that situation. Now you know that all the strength, courage and determination is within you.

Warning: Don't cheat yourself by just reading this then forgetting about it the next day. It took me too long to realise that only taking action and doing something gets results. Only you can do what you need to do so make a commitment to yourself that you are going to do whatever it takes to get the results you want. Don't mess about anymore. Don't waste time. Don't live with regrets.

Free Membership Offer

Sign up as a FREE member
at *www.supermummy.com*
and get instant access to the
best online mumpreneur tips,
strategies, resources and
success coaching.

Join now at...
www.supermummy.com

About the Author

Mel McGee is a Mumpreneur Coach and founder of *www.supermummy.com* - the UK's first online coaching and marketing service exclusively for aspiring and established mumpreneurs. Supermummy is an innovative company that helps mums to grow their business and themselves and create their ideal lifestyle business. Mel is an NLP Master Practitioner and a member of the Information Marketing Association. She lives in  Herefordshire, UK with her husband and 3 young children where she runs her successful international online business around family life.

Glossary of Terms

Autoresponder – an automatic response sent through software.

Blog – a kind of online journal.

Coaching – Advice which helps you to solve your own problems by implementing your own solutions.

Conversion rate – the number of visitors signing up or buying compared to total number of website visitors.

Copywriting – promotional words used to sell a product or service.

E-book – A digital file that can be downloaded electronically through the Internet.

E-zine – A newsletter delivered by e-mail either as text or HTML.

Freebie – Free information.

HTML – Computer language that is used to create pages for use on the Internet.

Information marketing – selling specialised and expert information in various combinations.

Lead generation - A process of identifying people in your target market who are interested in gaining more information about your product or service.

Multi-step marketing – a process of contacting prospects and customers on a regular basis.

Mumpreneur – A mum and an entrepreneur. A Supermummy!

Niche – A group of people with similar interests or demographics.

NLP – Abbreviation for Neuro Linguistic Programming that is based in modelling the excellence in others.

Outsourcing – paying for the skill and expertise of others to help you accomplish tasks.

Prospect – a person who has shown interest in your product or service.

Special report - free information available as an automatic download.

Shopping Cart – Software that allows you to take orders online and automate some processes.

Teleseminar – A conference call used as a way to share information and market a product or service.

Upsell – offering a higher priced product, service or package at the point of sale.

Essential Reading

Robbins, Tony, *Awaken The Giant Within*, Simon & Schuster, 1992

Kennedy, Dan, *No B.S Business Success*, Entrepreneur Press, 2004

Horn, Sam, *POP! Stand Out in Any Crowd*, Perigee, 2006

Ferris, Tim, *The 4 Hour Work Week*, Crown Publishers, 2007

SECRETS

OF SUCCESSFUL
WOMEN
ENTREPRENEURS

HOW TEN LEADING BUSINESS WOMEN
TURNED A GOOD IDEA INTO A FORTUNE

linda bennett glenda stone geetie singh penny streeter josephine carpenter

michelle mone yvonne thompson helen swaby marilyn orcharton julie meyer

SUE STOCKDALE

www.bookshaker.com

THE GORILLAS WANT BANANAS

The Lean Marketing™ Handbook for Small Expert Businesses

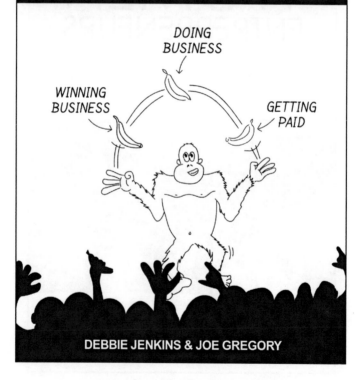

DOING BUSINESS

WINNING BUSINESS

GETTING PAID

DEBBIE JENKINS & JOE GREGORY

www.bookshaker.com

brightermarketing

THE
brighter
marketing
bible
FOR SMALL BUSINESSES

joanne morley | siobhan lees

www.bookshaker.com

GET
NOTICED

HOW TO BOOST YOUR
SMALL BUSINESS PROFILE
IN 30 DAYS OR LESS
PAULA GARDNER

www.bookshaker.com

Lightning Source UK Ltd.
Milton Keynes UK
07 October 2009

144639UK00001B/16/P